Honest Thieves

John L. Moore, Apprentice Seaman

Honest Thieves

The Diary of a Tangier Smuggler

by
John L. Moore

"I like a smuggler – he is the only honest thief."
—Charles Lamb

THE DARWIN PRESS, INC.
Princeton, New Jersey
2010

Publisher's Cataloging-In-Publication Data
(Prepared by The Donohue Group, Inc.)

Moore, John Lyon.
Honest thieves : the diary of a Tangier smuggler /
by John Lyon Moore.
p. : ill., maps, ports. ; cm.
ISBN: 978-0-87850-180-9

1. Moore, John Lyon—Diaries. 2. Smugglers—Morocco—Tangier—Biography. 3. Smuggling—Morocco—Tangier. 4. Tangier (Morocco)—History—20th century. I. Title.

HJ7095.Z5 M66 2010
364.133/09642/092 2010923366

Darwin® Books are printed on acid-free paper and meet the guidelines for permanence and durability of the Committee on production guidelines for Book Longevity of the Council on Library Resources. The paper used in this publication meets the minimum requirements of the American National Standard for Information Sciences—Permanence of Paper for Printed Library Materials, ANSI Z39.48-1992.

Published by:
The Darwin Press, Inc., Princeton, NJ 08543-2202 USA

Printed in the United States of America

Contents

N
W
E
S
250 MI
300 KM
FRANCE
Bordeaux
Bay of Biscay
Cape Ortegal
Santander
Cape Finisterre
Vigo Bay
Bayona
Oporto
Barcelona
Madrid
SPAIN
PORTUGAL
Burling Islands (Berlenga)
Lisbon
Palma
Mediterranean Sea
Cape Saint Vincent
Cape Sagres
Barbary Coast
SPAIN
Gibraltar
Cape Trafalgar
Algeciras
Strait of Gibraltar
Cape Tarifa
Cape Malabata
Ceuta
Cape Spartel
Tangier
MOROCCO
Port Lyautey (Kenitra)
Rabat
Casablanca
MOROCCO
Atlas Mts.

Map 1.

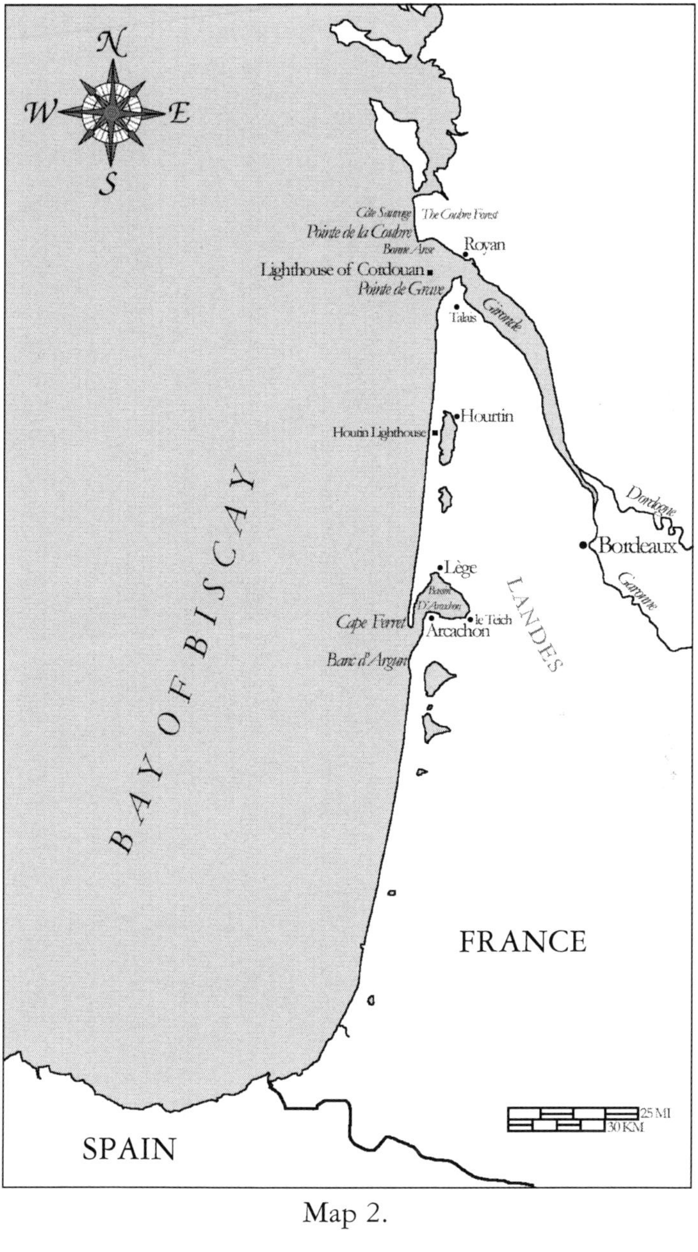
N
W
E
S
Côte Sauvage
The Coubre Forest
Pointe de la Coubre
Royan
Lighthouse of Cordouan
Pointe de Grave
Talais
Gironde
Hourtin
Hourtin Lighthouse
BAY OF BISCAY
Dordogne
Bordeaux
Garonne
Lège
LANDES
Cape Ferret
Arcachon
le Teich
Banc d'Arguin
FRANCE
25 MI
30 KM
SPAIN

Map 2.

Model of the *Seac* built by John L. Moore.

Foreword

In the 1940s and 1950s Tangier was a city of 125,000 souls—a city administered by a Committee representing eight foreign nations, including the United States. Established in 1925 as an International Zone of 225 square miles on the south shore of the Straits of Gibraltar, at the tip of what is now Morocco, the city was said to be "a den of thieves disguised as a noble experiment in international government." That is to say, this intriguing city that many viewed as being a safe haven for different levels of prosperous occupations—including among them: banking, trade, and smuggling—was in a real sense a "free city," with the Committee turning a blind eye to much of the contraband activity. In the mid-20th century, a preoccupation for survival turned to smuggling: gold, drugs, cigarettes—contraband of all kinds, including human beings.

Tangier boasted an indigenous population of native Moors and Jews, Spanish and French, as well as British and Dutch, and a considerable number of disaffected European and American expatriates.* Like the literary types who invaded Paris in the 1920s, the disaffected were not generally those who engaged in the smuggling operations or other doubtful occupations. Nor were the smugglers a majority of the motley mix of refugees. Among the refu-

*The city also maintained three different post offices—one each for the British, French, and Spanish. The American Legation, housed in the palace of the Medina in the old Moslem quarters, was both the post office and the headquarters for the American ex-pats.

gees was a small core of hardened criminals and others of less noble persuasion who came with the goal of doing whatever it would take to claim their fortune, and Tangier was a prime target for these types and for their activities. Among the smaller minority of others, however, were smugglers lured by the atmosphere of adventure—the romantics who wanted to enjoy life in an "open" city, who were attracted by the soft whiff of danger and wished to taste it, who wanted to be free. One of those American adventurers tempted by the lure of Tangier was John Lyon Moore.

John grew up in Orange, New Jersey. He and I were next-door neighbors for a number of years during our childhood. Although a year younger than I, John treated me as a brother. He had a sense of adventure, and as youngsters we shared many things in common; our escapades still live in my memory.

When we were teenagers, John and I joined the Montclair Mounted Troop, led by and large by West Point grads in the Army Reserve. There were two women's troops and three men's troops that marched and rode on different nights. We met weekly in West Orange, New Jersey, on top of Eagle Rock Avenue. John and I were Lance Corporals, and we loved to ride. On one occasion both the men and women troops were thrilled to march at the opening of the national horse show in Madison Square Garden.

On weekends we would rent horses from a local riding academy near Pal's cabin, a teenage hangout. We would also ride and parade them at Eagle Rock Reservation where one could hire a horse for an hour or two. We loved to gallop full steam and in single file, jumping over large logs and being careful not to fall off when brushing by small trees along the path. The owner of the stable did not appreciate our returning the horses all lathered up and sweaty from our galloping escapades.

To know John was to know a certain kind of fearlessness combined with a sense of humor that endeared him to his many friends. One such noteworthy example that I witnessed was in the form of a practical joke played on John that made newspaper headlines. Unbeknownst to John, some of his Seton Hall school pals and I signed him up as a contestant in the 1944 Newark News Golden Gloves boxing tournament. Not wanting to let his friends down, he agreed to rise to the challenge. His first scheduled fight happened to take place on his 17th birthday. Fighting in the light-heavyweight division at 175 pounds, he met his challenge in James Henry, a fearsome opponent. With a little more than a minute gone in the first round, John knocked out his opponent with one (lucky?) punch—to the immense relief of his jokester pals who had entered him in the tournament. To which the *Newark Evening News* commented in a bold headline: "Jokers Entered John Moore in Golden Gloves Tourney, but Joke's on Them." Unfortunately, John was outpointed in the quarter finals by his next opponent, while giving everyone a good account of his novice boxing skills.

John and I shared a common love for the sea, and we enjoyed one summer of sailing at the New Jersey shore. In the following year (1945) John graduated from Seton Hall prep, joined the U.S. Navy, and was stationed at Bainbridge Naval Station.

Meanwhile, I was sailing as a cadet/midshipman from the United States Merchant Marine Academy (USMMA), fulfilling the required six months in the Pacific theater and then another 18 months as a deck officer. Some years later, I served two more years on active Navy duty as Ships Medical Officer (1955–1957). My longing for sea time was fulfilled at the completion of 64 Atlantic crossings, which happily resulted in my Navy discharge. John, however, missed the adventure of being onboard ship abroad.

After the war John attended Georgetown University, majoring in history and political science and graduating in the spring of 1950. Seeking new fields to conquer, he was restless, craving travel and the romance of spending time abroad in another culture. North Africa was in the news at the time, and appealed to John's sense of the foreign and exotic.

In late April 1950 John booked one-way passage aboard the M/S "Fernhill," destination Casablanca in what was then French Morocco. John's parents and I and a few friends, along with his sweetheart, Marg, saw him off. Lured by his wanderlust and fueled by his love for the sea, he began his trip into the unknown, a trip filled with possibilities.

And that is where his story begins.

William F. Haynes, Jr., M.D.

Chapter One

The Barbary Coast

Some said Tangier had the smell of money and maybe it *was* the twenty tons of gold bullion in the bank vaults under the city. To me, in the Spring of 1950, it just smelled of wood smoke and mimosa. It had been a long haul on trains, trucks, and busses from French Morocco into Spanish Morocco at Ksar-el-Kebir, where I was strip searched and then through the mountains to Tangier. In Marrakech I'd been told that Tangier was where the action was. In Casablanca Mike Derby called it a racketeer's town, and in Port Lyautey they said it was a place where an American could get work.

I knew bits and pieces about the place. The city was 2,500 years old and was situated in an International Zone on the Africa side of the Straits of Gibraltar and was run by eight nations including the United States. During the War in Europe and North Africa, Tangier was the espionage center of the western Mediterranean. Now it was a den of thieves thriving on the misfortunes of the world at large, and home to army deserters, political refugees, ex-Nazis, and remittance men. Plus the largest band of sea smugglers who ever got together in one place. And this crowd wasn't deprived of diversions. Forty-two brothels were licensed and there were probably three times as many unlicensed, male and female. No one ever succeeded in counting the bars. Absinthe, banned in the civilized world, was legal here, and *kif*, the local hashish, was sold at any tobacco stand. The town's favorite candy was *majoun*, a confection of honey, dates, and marijuana. A fun kind of place, but the city also did business.

Every conceivable type of contraband was carried out of Tangier and smuggled into Europe. This included nylons, medicine, gold, guns, and currency. Refugees were moved and so on occasion were drugs. But the real money cargo was American cigarettes. They came tax- and duty-free from the United States, went into a bonded warehouse in Tangier's port, and from there were shipped to Spain, France, or Italy in the boats of the smuggling armada.

The boats ran the gamut of sailing yachts, fishing boats, and every variety of retired small naval vessels, mostly late of the British Admiralty: sub chasers, harbor craft, convoy escorts, and minesweepers. Crews were a mixed bag of Europeans, British, Maltese, and a few Americans. While a couple of boats, known as *scorpions* to the British, were owned by Americans and a few more by Spaniards or Gibraltarians, almost all were of British Registry as cargo carrying yachts. They had British captains or mates and sailed under the red merchant ensign of the United Kingdom. Mob boss Lucky Luciano, in exile in Naples for four years now, was said to have more than a passing interest in the operation, and Tangier's smuggling boats were referred to in the press as "Lucky's Sixth Fleet."

I didn't know anyone in Tangier, and when I got there the only names I had were the Parade Bar, Dean's Bar, and the Hotel Cecil. It was late evening when I took a room at the Cecil, which was a waterfront relic but cheap. I changed my shirt and set out up the hill to find a drink. I found one on the ground floor of an apartment building off the Boulevard Pasteur in the Parade Bar. The Parade had a touch of both class and glitz, zebra upholstery, soft lights, and a pink silk canopy over the bar. A man who introduced himself to me as Bill Chase, one of the owners, poured me a gin.

"Will it be cash or on your account?"

"I don't think I have an account. I've been in Tangier about an hour and a half."

"Long enough. It's on your account and you pay when its convenient. Welcome to Tangier." I knew right then I was going to like this town.

By midnight the place was pretty well full, mostly expatriate Americans and staff and Marines from the U.S. Legation. I met a lot of people that night and spent most of the evening with three in particular.

Bill Bird, probably in his sixties, was publisher of the *Tangier Gazette*. In the 1920s he had operated his own wire service in Paris and had founded Three Mountains Press, publishing Ezra Pound, William Carlos Williams, Ford Maddox Ford, and Ernest Hemingway. With encouragement from Bill Chase and his partner Jay Haselwood, Bird talked about his experiences with his writers and with Sylvia Beach, Gertrude Stein, and James Joyce. "I read a galley copy of *Ulysses* and wrote Joyce a note with my comments. You know, he wrote back that I was the only person to that point who understood what he was doing." Pretty heavy stuff, I thought.

In 1924 Bird was Hemingway's first publisher. Bird's Three Mountains Press published *In Our Time,* and for a number of years Bird was probably Hemingway's closest friend, travelling with him in Spain, Italy, and Germany. More than once Bird has been identified as the source of Jake Barnes' mannerisms in *The Sun Also Rises*.

With a lull in the literary talk I asked Bird and Chase about the smuggling business, and with that they introduced me to Bud Priest.

Priest looked more than a little bit like Bogart and was supposed to be the toughest man in that part of Africa, at least the toughest American. He was maybe in his forties, but who could tell. Someone said he would have to be eighty to have done everything he was supposed to have done: a miner in Alaska, a construction boss and cat-skinner on the Gold Coast, and a ranch hand in Montana. But he was friendly and willing to educate a newcomer. The boat runs, he told me, were usually about ten days and were mainly in the Mediterranean to the east coast of Spain, or the Italian and French rivieras at Portofino, Cape d'Antibes, and Villefranche-sur-Mer. Cigarettes in bond in Tangier cost less than seven cents a pack and sold off the coast of Europe for six times that. "Everything about the business is legal, or at least it should be," Priest told me, "until you get to the point of delivery. You see, you used to have a three-mile jurisdiction limit in territorial waters but all of them—the Spanish, French, and Italians—took it on themselves to extend it to twelve. And even at that the bastards don't play fair. They've got the edge on us anyway, with their radar and fast patrol boats and machine guns, but they'll chase you and take shots at you no matter where you are, international waters be damned. The Spanish have a fleet of German E-boats parked at both ends of the Straits in Tarifa and Ceuta, and if they see you they'll shoot you up almost before you're away from the dock." Another problem closer to home, he told me, were the spies and informers who sold traffic information to the enemy, as well as the consular intelligence people and Interpol, which was the international police organization that had an active presence in Tangier.

Priest talked about his own boat, the *Sayon,* which Chase said was the biggest and snappiest motor yacht in the trade. "*Sayon* is over in Algeciras for repairs right now, that's across the Straits by Gib. The *levanter* blew her on the rocks a month ago and she's really banged up. Now she's giving me one headache after another." (The *levanter* is the fierce east wind, much like the mistral further east, that blows through the Straits periodically without warning and raises holy hell in the port.) But Priest's headaches now were crew problems. "With some of my boys here and some in Spain and Gib, I can't keep them sober and I can't keep them out of jail. Last week I had a Swede of mine locked up in La Linea and the same time my engineer was locked up in Gib. They're driving me nuts."

A woman at the bar turned to Priest and asked when he thought he'd have *Sayon* running again. "I have no idea, the way those Spaniards work." He introduced me to Nancy Nicholson, a good looking American blonde. Priest said things were so uncertain with *Sayon* that he was seriously thinking about buying another boat. "I looked at a 'Harry Duffy,' but it's too much money." In answer to my puzzled look he explained that this was Brit Navy lingo for harbor duty craft. "They're pretty much like the MFV, the motor fishing vessel."

Nancy asked if there was any word yet on Pierre and, turning to me, told me that Pierre Coupay was a French doctor turned smuggler and a crew member on the *Sun-*

shine, a trading sloop that was machine-gunned to pieces 15 miles off the Italian coast near Genoa. Her 300 cases were confiscated or destroyed and Pierre was in jail with the rest of the crew and his Captain. "Still no word," Priest replied, "but Charlie Miranda thinks he'll be out soon and Charlie probably knows."

"His wife still living on his boat with Henri?" asked Nancy.

"Yes, but Pierre and Henri and the wife were living on the boat together before he went on *Sunshine*. Pierre and Henri are best friends."

"Sure," she said, "and best friends share."

We drank and talked 'til near dawn. I learned about smuggling from Priest and listened to Nancy on bull-fighting. I overheard her earlier conversation with two Legation Marines, and already knew that her two interests in life were smuggling boats and bullfights. Every Sunday during the season she was in Tetuan in the Spanish Zone or across the Straits in La Linea or Algeciras. She had a sexual thing about bullfighters and the Mexican Carlos Aruzza was her current favorite. A month before she had seen him perform in Seville and he took two ears and a tail in two successive fights. She wondered aloud what kind of a lover he'd be. She wondered too what her husband would think about bullfighting, and I asked her where he was, this husband. "Back in Philadelphia playing left field for the Phillies," she said.

"Is he any good?" I asked her.

"He's good enough. Back in '44, when he was with the Cubs, the Giants put him on base with an intentional walk."

"So?"

"They did it with the bases loaded—you can look it up. Bill was good."

I left the Parade with directions from Priest about where I could exchange some currency the next day and with a date to meet Nancy for lunch. Going out I passed Truman Capote in the hallway coming in.

At noon I was in the Soco Chico, the real heart of the city and the most interesting half acre of real estate in Africa. In name "The Little Market," it was really a courtyard in the old city next to the Casbah, dominated by the Fuentes Hotel and the Spanish Post Office and flanked with open-fronted cafés. Here, more than anywhere else in Tangier, you found the castaways and misfits—army deserters, old time Trotskyites, criminals, and hustlers—all escaping their pasts in a haze of *kif* and alcohol. I had a sandwich with Nancy on the terrace of the Café Central, learned that she was also staying at the Cecil, and together we headed up the narrow way of Es Siaghines, the street of the moneychangers, connecting the Soco Chico and the larger Soco Grande.

Tangier had no taxes or money restrictions and had no currency of its own to protect. In fact it had become the backwater of paper money. With no controls and with no national bank interested in exchanging new bills for old, money circulated until it literally fell apart. A game I learned to play was not to be the last man stuck with a crumbling five peseta note that no one would take. Five pesetas was worth about fifteen cents American. In French establishments, prices were in French francs and in Spanish places in pesetas, but pounds, lira, and dollars were accepted as well. On the sidewalks on both sides of the street there were 80 or more money-exchange stands, some of them only pushcarts or a couple of orange crates, each with a chalk board showing the rates. In this alley, as much as in Tangier's 85 banking houses, the money trading helped determine exchange rates in New York, London, and Paris. Most people in Tangier carried two or three kinds of currency in their pockets and three or four exchange rates in their heads. This was an acquired talent as rates changed rapidly, often several times in an hour, and the word passed through the city like ball-game scores during a World Series. After changing some bills at what I was happy to believe was the best rate available, we moved on to Dean's.

The doorway to Dean's Bar in the rue Sud America was almost completely blocked by a cream-colored Cadillac parked halfway on the narrow sidewalk. Inside, the barroom was filled with afternoon drinkers, including a British Admiral over from Gibraltar, an Italian princess and a pair from the Moroccan nationalist Istiqlal movement who were hunted in the French and Spanish territories but safe here in the International Zone. And plenty of gentlemen from the contraband trade. But even in this company the shop's proprietor was hands down the most interesting person in the place. Joseph Dean, a leather-faced Anglo-Egyptian octoroon with an Oxford accent, was a lover of the arts, a spy through two world wars, and the best known saloon keeper in Africa. Part of his fame lay in his ability to eavesdrop on as many as three conversations at a time, never mind they were in three different languages. Dean was fluent in six. His bar was open from noon until two or three and then from eight until he was in the mood to close, maybe eleven or maybe five in the morning, depending on whether his patrons bored him or amused him.

Nancy bypassed the Admiral and Princess and introduced me to some of the smugglers. The car outside belonged to "Nylon" Sid Paley from Jersey City, now the operator of a panty factory in Tangier and the owner of the motorship *Laloun.* Henri Gillette was the Belgian who was Pierre's friend and Pierre's wife's friend, discussed the night before at Parade. I also met Bill Lacey, a hard-looking Irishman, and Byron Yates, a mild looking American.

Bill Lacey was First Mate on *Seac* and By Yates was assistant to an Arab shipchandler in the rue Cadiz down in the port. Conversation at the bar was mainly about seamen and boats that were in port, boats with names like *Sonning*, *Seac*, *Rifrock,* and *Porcupine*, and at least one boat that wasn't in port. The *Thetis* had "disappeared away" from the harbor along with its just-loaded cargo of 220 cases. The incident was mentioned in passing, but when I asked for details Lacey said, "It's better not to know," and we talked about other things.

"Martin brought in his *Great Scot* last night," Yates said, "a fine looking boat."

"God," said Nancy, "I'd give anything to have that boat, or any boat. I'd even look at the 'Harry Duffy' Bud Priest was talking about but if it's too much money for him, I'd be wasting my time."

"You need a boat, and I need to be a captain," Lacey growled, "I'm bloody-well tired of being a mate." This was a lament I'd hear from Lacey often in the days to come.

"And I need a job," I added, "my money is just about gone."

"If money's your problem," said Yates, "maybe you ought to get to know the lady at the end of the bar." I took a look and saw he was probably right. The lady was Barbara Hutton, said to be the richest woman in the world. They told me she had a home—one of many—in the Casbah, the Palace Sidi Hosni, and she stayed in Tangier a month or two every year with her collection of Manets, El Grecos, and husbands or, as now, lovers. I met her a few days later but having a couple of drinks with her at Dean's had no effect whatsoever on my finances. She was a nice lady but was bitter about the way she was treated in the press. She had recently either invested in or donated money to an English language newspaper in Rome, "and all they have to say is I'm using my money again to buy influence. Whatever I do with my damned money I'm always wrong it seems."

One day in Tangier . . . and I had any number of pals. That evening Lacey and Yates and I had steaks and hot sauce in a place in back of the Soco Chico and from there rambled on to the Mar Chico, the Aduana, and the Puerto del Sol—Spanish taverns near the entrance to the port. Each had the head of a bull on the wall and Manolete's picture enshrined over the bar. The Mar Chico was the best of them, a single low-ceilinged room of old timbers and smoke-darkened plaster. Here they chalk the price of your drinks on the zinc bar and it never comes to very much. These places were hangouts for the men off the boats, and we were joined in the Mar Chico by Elliot Forrest and a Dane named Hans. Forrest was from the Bronx and maybe thirty years old, a guy who'd been around the block a couple of times. In 1948 he'd been in the papers for trying to spirit a war surplus sub-chaser out of New

York for Tangier—that and a load of guns he hoped to get to the Stern Gang in Palestine. Then he'd been a nightclub operator and more recently the "contact man" or supercargo on a couple of runs aboard *Seac* with Lacey.

The talk continued to be about boats, captains, and crews. Just about all the smuggling fleet was in port because of the full moon. To be on the rendezvous, where cargo was off-loaded to be put ashore, or even to be running, under anything more than a quarter moon was to invite serious trouble from coast-watchers and customs patrols.

"A lot of boats out there," said Forrest, "and a lot of cargo and a lot of money."

In one of the bars Captain Goldy stopped to say hello and have a drink with us. He was a small aging Brit with a white goatee and a natty beret. He was sailing around the world on a small sloop at his own pace and had interrupted his voyage to do a couple of cigarette runs. When Goldy left, Lacey continued to ponder the ways he might get a command of his own. "I keep wondering about the *Antonina*," he said to Yates. "Maybe White will be running her again and need a skipper."

"She's a bad boat, Bill," said Hans, adding that "the police and customs tear her apart in every port she makes. She has a bad reputation and always will have. She was a drug runner once, you know, and she'll always be trouble. I'd be careful getting involved with her."

Lacey listened to Hans knowing full well that he was not timid by nature. Only a few years earlier he had been with the Danish resistance, stringing wires across dark roads, neck high for the benefit of Wehrmacht motorcycle couriers. But Lacey went on to tell us more news about

Antonina, a 112-foot Fairmile convoy escort, fast and trim and "a lovely boat." She was owned by an Englishman named White who no longer had the stomach to run her himself. She was in port now at Villefranche on the Riviera. "Just sitting there, not bringing in a damned quid. A bloody shame is what it is."

I spent part of the next few days looking for a job on one of the boats, but without any luck, and the rest of the time hanging out with Yates and Lacey and their friends at a sidewalk table in front of the Puerta Café, conveniently next door to the shipchandler's office of Hadj Mohamed Agzenai where Lacey worked. His was hardly a job to put a strain on a man.

Tangier harbor had suffered centuries of neglect and was so silted up that few ships of any size made it a port of call. By's job consisted of occasionally meeting a ship, buying the Captain or Mate a drink or two, and writing up whatever order he could get. His business was more with the port's contraband runners who he said were truly gentlemen.

"I'm fond of this job," he continued, "I think I've found my place in life. It's really like Joseph Conrad said, 'a beautiful and humane occupation'."

Through each afternoon the crate of empty Stork beer bottles next to our table filled up, was emptied, and filled again. Stork was not only Casablanca's best bar, it was Casablanca's cheapest. When Nancy joined us her drink was Tio Pepe sherry, also cheap. At night it was usually the Parade or Dean's for us.

I was living pretty well, I thought, for someone who was broke, but then there were ways to economize. There was one place in a back-alley doorway where they sold a shot of Terry brandy for two cents American and another place in the Casbah that put out a lunch, with soup and a Coke bottle of red wine, for nine cents.

George was a regular at Dean's and I got to know him well but never learned his last name. He was a fat Englishman, a retired journalist of some sort, who knew more than anyone ever needed to know about the history of sea smuggling, the *old* history of sea smuggling. I spent the better part of a night letting George take me back to the eighteenth century and the owlers of Romney Marsh, Rattenbury and the Hawkhurst Gang of his beloved coast of Cornwall. "Oh, they were real rascals, those moon-rakers, Dick of the Downs, and the rest of them. There's none of their likes today in this place, I can tell you, not when it comes to seamanship. Ah, how does it go now: 'A beacon's gleam on the clifftop edge,/where no light has ever been/and the smugglers lurk in their secret cove/as they flash the lugger in'."

Poetry or prose, he knew his subject. I guessed he had written articles about it at one time or another.

"There's little new today in this contraband business," he said. "It was all the same 200 years ago. Roscoff on the Channel was the free port then; now it's Tangier. Boats clearing for false ports? Nothing new. They all cry about the 12-mile limit, but that's nothing new either. Two hundred years ago the limit was four leagues and that, my boy, was 12 miles." He continued his lecture into the night, evoking images of the sea smuggler's forebear standing at his helm, reckless and hardy in the teeth of the gale. I left George that night wondering if perhaps the profession had indeed fallen on gentler days. I was soon to find out.

In those first days I got to know any number of people from Tangier's cadre of smugglers, writers and diplomats, and just plain folks like Nancy and Miss Hutton. But I was aware too of the shadowy individuals who lived in a kind of twilight world.

Every day and every night you could run into Albert the Portuguese in some part of the city. Albert was a *simsar* by trade, which translated into pest. A breed that thrives in the ports of Africa and Asia, he was a professional go-between. Every day he'd introduce you to someone you had no interest in knowing and would put you on to some commodity you had no interest in acquiring: two dozen rubber rafts one day, the next day a sublet apartment in the Casbah.

Peter was another one, an English remittance man, paid by someone to stay far away from home. He lived with a kind of male nurse or companion and seemed afflicted with either a neurosis or an addiction, maybe both.

And Paul. I met Paul one evening when we shared a table outside the Café de Paris on the Place de France. In accented English he told me he was from Luxembourg and had deserted from the French Foreign Legion. He had done his time in Indochina, fought Giap in the Tonkin Delta in 1948 with the 13th Demi-Brigade and was later with the 1st Parachute Battalion. He had taken off from his post in Oujda when he got orders to report to Sidi Bel Abbes for shipment to the Libyan desert for a year of camel police duty. Paul was a frightened man because this, he told me, was his second desertion. The first time he returned and served his 60 days in confinement, but a second time would be different. "This time if I go back, or if they take me back, it means the penal battalion at Colomb-Béchar and that's a place where you die. Twenty years ago the Legion gave Berber tribesmen a bounty for bringing in deserters, twenty francs alive, 100 francs for a man's head. The bounty may have changed but the Legion's thinking hasn't."

Later on I drank with Paul a couple of times in the Soco and at Djory's, and he told me he was really German and had been in Rommel's Afrika Corps. No surprise, the Legion was then between 40 and 80 percent German. My other friends who got to know Paul agreed he was German but thought it more than likely he had been S.S. and had more to worry about than being returned to the Legion. After a couple of weeks he disappeared.

Then one night Nancy threw a dinner party. The terrace of the Cecil was in the same state of genteel decay as the rest of the hotel and this looked to be the first dinner party it had seen in some decades. Grass grew through the cracks in the concrete paving and the late dusk just began to hide the nearby litter and construction debris. But with full darkness the view was spectacular: the harbor, the Straits, and 20 miles across were the lights of Spain at Tarifa and Cape Camarinal. "The light there to the left is Punta Marroqui, the most southerly point in Europe," Nancy told me.

Besides me, her guests were Lacey, Yates, two Americans named Junior Fuller and Bob Gates, an Irishman named O'Brien, and two very chic French women, Françoise and Michele. The terrace itself may have seen better days but the dinner party was elegant indeed. The long table with its white cloth, linen napkins, and fine china sparkled with three sets of crystal candelabra. The couscous with mutton was prepared as it should be and was served with a superior red wine. And the company was interesting.

Junior Fuller was big and muscle-bound, and generously tattooed; he arrived on a motorcycle. He talked of his days running refugees out of Shanghai to the Philippines and was every inch an old China Hand. He also told of a few experiences with his Portuguese girl-friend Piggy (a girl who worked in Freddy's night club up on the hill) that weren't in the best taste. I asked him if I understood her name to be "Peggy," but he said, "no, Piggy."

At one point I thought I heard Gates tell one of the French girls his name was Yates, but decided I heard wrong. Byron Yates across the table apparently didn't hear this and anyway seemed to be avoiding any conversation with Gates, though I was sure they knew each other.

O'Brien was friendly enough, if a bit of an airhead; his only talk was of his point-to-point racing back home in the Wicklow Hills. I learned later that Fuller and O'Brien had a business of sorts taking automobiles into Spain and selling them there illegally with forged papers.

Predictably most of the conversation through dinner and afterwards was steered by Nancy to bullfights and smuggling. Over a couple of bottles of Terry brandy and the last of the wine, we sat in the flickering light of the candles, and after O'Brien and Fuller left with the French girls, we again discussed how Lacey might become a captain and how Nancy might acquire a boat. It all called to mind something else Conrad had written about the hopes, dangers, and enterprises of those who inhabit the dark places of the sea.

"If I can't buy a boat, there's another way to get one," Nancy said, getting our attention. Everyone seemed to know what was coming.

"Steal one," said Lacey.

"There's one right over there in Algeciras and a Fairmile at that. Nailed by a Spanish patrol boat two months ago. I don't know her name, but I've seen her. She's just lying tied up to a dock; 'impounded' I think they call it. And the only guard they have on her is one old man who looks like a civilian and is drunk half the time. I doubt he even has a gun."

Nancy went on to sketch out the details of a heist that would only require cutting mooring lines and having another boat tow the prize back to Tangier, or at worst to Gibraltar. "If somebody could take *Thetis* right out of our port here, this job shouldn't be all that hard."

"You sound like Forrest," Lacey told her, "he's the one who talks about getting a boat or a cargo on the cheap." That some might consider it a crime to steal a boat never seemed to occur to Nancy. As a matter of fact, the actual concept of crime seemed to be far from the minds of anyone in this town. Certainly no one thought of smuggling as a crime, and this was understandable in as much as 90 percent of each run was technically legal. And for the sinful reputation it had, Tangier itself was surprisingly crime-free. There was mention of this when the conversation turned to the subject of murder, a topic prompted perhaps by Nancy's unspoken plans for the Spanish watchman.

"I don't believe we've officially had a murder here since the Countess," said Yates. "Of course, there was that fellow they found in the Casbah last year with a knife in his back, but the Police called that one a suicide."

The Countess he was referring to was Countess Magda d'Omduran, at one time or another a professional spy, mistress of a millionaire, and wife of an Arabian Pasha.

When she disappeared from her yacht in the harbor, she was living with a former Gestapo officer who was about to run a quantity of South African gold dust to France. Her body, when it washed ashore, had a smashed head and the German claimed she'd had a fall, and he put her body over the side. The Court didn't think so and he got 25 years.

Nancy returned to the boat in Spain. "That Fairmile is do-able," she insisted.

"Listen," said Lacey, "this may not be the best time for that kind of thing. Charlie Miranda says the whole business is going to take a turn and things are likely to get very rough." There was that name again, and this time I asked who was Charlie Miranda.

"Depends on who you talk to," said Lacey. "Ask Charlie and he's in import and export. Others will tell you that it may be import and export but he makes a bloody lot of trips to see the man in Naples."

"The man in Naples?"

"Charlie Lucky—Lucky Luciano." End of topic and back to boats and people other than Miranda and Luciano until it got very late and the party was over.

The next day I arrived at Yates' office just as Lacey was leaving, an envelope in hand. "I'm leaving on a run but I've written to White in France," he said, "and proposed a sort of syndicate to run *Antonina*. I told him we wanted half the profits with the books kept here, not in Villefranche, and complete freedom to run her where we want and with whatever cargo we want." Lacey didn't say who the "we" were who would make up his syndicate. "With me being Captain, of course," he added.

"Of course," Yates repeated with a smile, and I asked him a question that seemed peculiar: "Have you thought about where you're going to mail it?" The question was not so peculiar because I had learned that Tangier had three separate postal services, each complete with their own stamps and post office. The British had a post office and so did the French and the Spanish. The Spanish post office in the Soco had the cheapest postage rates, but was regarded as too unreliable to use for serious correspondence. The rumor was that, if you were involved with contraband and used the French post office, you ran the risk of having your mail opened. Lacey said he was going up to the British post office on the Boulevard Pasteur.

After Lacey left I had a beer with Yates and was about to leave myself when Yates said, "I'll see you later at the Legation."

"You will? Why would I be at the Legation?"

"Because," Yates explained to me patiently, "today is the glorious anniversary of our independence and there will be the usual booze and food extravaganza at Uncle's expense. It's at seven o'clock, and I'm sure you wouldn't want to miss it and be thought unpatriotic." I had not only lost track of the days but had almost bypassed the 4th of July.

At seven o'clock, splendid in my last clean shirt, I gave a nod to the Marine sentry in his dress blues and entered Diplomat Country to get my justly due ration of free booze and free food. After a half hour and three very quick drinks I found Bud Priest and asked him one more time if he couldn't use me on *Sayon*. One more time he said he couldn't, not just yet, but made the suggestion that I go see MacQueen. "His boat is *Seac* and he's getting ready to go. I heard this morning he'll take on one more hand. He'd be worth talking to."

An hour later I got an Arab to row me across the inner port, and with permission from someone I couldn't see I climbed aboard *Seac*. I recalled then that this was the boat in which Lacey sailed as mate and Forrest had sailed as contact man. A voice from the deck cabin, more growl than invitation, told me to come inside. I did and I met Andrew MacQueen.

McQueen was middle-aged, paunchy, and well on his way to being bald. There were few signs that life had treated him either too well or too badly, but one look at the man and you knew he was someone who could handle himself and handle others. MacQueen had been to sea with the Royal Navy in two wars and in between earned a reputation in North Scotland as a motorcycle racer. I introduced myself and he nodded toward the second man in the cabin, "My son, Bosun." Andrew MacQueen, Jr. was in his twenties and built like a medium-sized mountain.

"Can you use me in your crew?" I asked without wasting time. "I heard you could use another hand and I'm looking for work."

"I maybe could use you—you talk like a Yank."

"I am."

"American passport?" I said yes, I had one.

"Fine," he said, "You're hired." I waited for the questions about experience, but there were none. Nor was there any discussion about pay or about anything else. MacQueen was a man of few words. I had my job and I left well enough alone.

"We'll be here tomorrow on the night tide, and you can call me Mac if you want, we're not much on formalities on *Seac*."

But then I didn't leave well enough alone and almost blew it. I should have known better but asked him, "Where is it we're going?"

MacQueen and Bosun looked at each other and then at me like I was from some other planet. When Mac spoke it was in a barely audible voice, but right in my face: "That, lad, is a question that does not get asked and a question that does not get answered. You'll know where you're going when you get there." He told me to meet him the next morning and I left *Seac* in a hurry, glad to still have my job. The next day I gathered my stuff, settled my bill at the Cecil with money borrowed from Yates, and said my good-byes to him and Hans. And to Bud Priest, with my thanks, when I saw him in the Place de France. I met MacQueen at noon at the British Consulate and with more formality than I expected I signed Ships Articles of the Motor Yacht *Seac* and became, at least for awhile, a member of the British Merchant Navy. On the way back down to the Port, Mac said that Bill Lacey was his First Officer and I told him I knew Lacey. He told me that besides himself we'd be a crew of four, and that was all he told me.

At daybreak I got my first real look at the boat I would sail in. *Seac* was a 61-foot North Sea fishing boat built in 1944 for the British Admiralty and was designated an MFV for motor fishing vessel. She was made of wood, 50 tons gross, and had a broad beam and masts forward and aft. Not a particularly graceful boat, her lines spoke of seaworthiness rather than speed. But I was to learn that the "speedy smuggling fleet" in Tangier was mostly a myth generated by newspaper and magazine writers. With the exception of a few convoy escort (probably submarine) chasers most of the boats had been converted from gasoline to diesel for economy. *Seac*'s engine was a four-cylinder Kelvin diesel that could push the boat to a top speed of nine knots, but only with a friendly current and wind and help from a jury-rigged sail. Her deck cabin served as Master's quarters, wardroom and mess, but for all of that it was hardly roomy. It had a bunk, a bench, and a table big enough for six men to eat at or play poker. The cabin's lockers were full of canned food and, I later discovered, some guns. The galley that was used at sea was a closet on the after end of the deck cabin with a two-burner primus stove, some pots, and our tin mess bowls and cups, but not enough room for the cook. Whoever cooked stood in the cabin and needed a long reach. The wheel house was forward of the deck cabin and elevated a couple of feet above deck level, a small place with a big wooden wheel and brass throttle as well as charts, pilot books, the ship's log, and a flare gun. Signal pennants and various other flags were stowed in a row of pigeon holes. Although she sailed under the Red Duster, Britain's merchant ensign, *Seac* also carried the white ensign of the Royal Navy and the blue ensign of the naval auxiliary in case circumstances required the use of either. She had Spanish, French, and Italian flags as well, and it wouldn't have surprised me if somewhere in the flag locker she had a burgee of the New York Yacht Club. False colors to deceive the enemy, a British sea tradition since before Nelson's day.

The only instruments she carried were a compass, a clock, and a barometer. No radio. The boat's saloon was below deck and forward, also two small sleeping cabins, a head and the main galley. There were chain and paint lockers in the forepeak. The forward galley was used now as a storage bin and had a sink, an old refrigerator that didn't work, and another primus stove. There was a good library of sea stories in the saloon, perhaps 20 or 30 books, but these were never accessible the first half of any run because the saloon and forward cabins were where the cargo was stowed and no one ever thought to get books out before the cigarettes were loaded. The engine room amidships was reached by a ladder aft of the wheel house, and another ladder-way aft of the deck cabin was our access to crew quarters. Deep in the stern with the racket of the propeller, the engine fumes, and the wet of the bilges there was a cabin with bunks for all of us except the Captain. There was another head back there and a spare bunk tucked in back of the ladder.

When I went aboard with MacQueen I found Bosun and Lacey and a little gray-haired lady busy clearing a clutter of stuff from the decks and stowing things in their proper places. I met Mrs. MacQueen and learned that smuggling on *Seac* was indeed a family affair. At her directions a hundred pounds of potatoes went into the spud locker aft of the galley and eggs and butter into lockers in the deck cabin; a garland of onions was tied to the aftermast where they'd be in the open air. We lashed four jerry cans of paraffin for the cooking stove to the gunnels by the wheel house. Satisfied we'd be properly fed, Mrs. MacQueen said goodbye and went ashore.

A week earlier, *Seac* had gone over to Gib to take on fuel oil and canned food. When all the stuff was stowed Lacey and I stripped the saloon bare for loading, cramming whatever was moveable into the forward galley.

We came on deck as our final crew member was coming aboard. It was my drinking friend from Dean's, Henri; in his Scotch burr, Mac called him "Henley." It was like old home week. By ten o'clock that night we had the boat's dinghy out of the water and tied on the roof of the deck cabin. Then I got my first taste of real work.

Weighing anchor on *Seac* was done without help from the motor winch on the forward deck, another item apparently not in working order. Where she lay in the inner port, *Seac* had two bow lines to the seawall and a hedge anchor dropped astern. The anchor cable ran the length of the deck to a hand windlass in the bow and was coated with a heavy mess of grease. Each of us took our turn cranking the windlass while the rest tugged and pulled on the slippery cable to guide it past the deck cabin and wheel house and get it on the spool. Hard work and messy. When the anchor was aboard we slipped the bow lines and Mac started the engine and backed her over to the wall by the Port Captain's office and the warehouse. We tied up and took a hose aboard to fill our water tanks. Mac went ashore to attend to manifests and clearance papers, and the rest of us kept busy fending off a horde of natives who wanted to climb aboard. We unscrewed the skylight over the saloon, and Bosun picked a half dozen of the likelier looking natives to help us with the loading. Already there were Arabs dragging cases of cigarettes out of the warehouse and piling them on the seawall.

We had just started to pass the first cases aboard when Henri Gillette, our missing crewman, hove into sight, and "sight" is the proper word for this fellow. The Belgian was wearing an oversized turtleneck sweater, a pair of blue jeans, turned down sea boots, and a red bandana. Even on the Tangier waterfront he was something to look at twice. Henri was in his thirties I guessed, of medium size, with a deceptively boyish face and a rather refined continental accent. He joined us at once in our work.

Most of our three hundred cases were out of the warehouse now and we hurried with the loading. Bosun and I worked below in the saloon and stowed the cases as they were handed down to us through the skylight. The hold was still full of the heat of the day, and before we were a hundred cases done our trousers were plastered to our bodies with sweat. We had long since shed our shirts. Some of the metal bands on the cases snapped loose and cut our hands. Already I thought there was less glamour to being a smuggler than I had originally supposed.

When the loading was done, the skylight secured, and the last of the Arabs paid off and chased away, Mac assembled us on the foredeck.

"Why a sailor must fill his belly with grog before he feels he can go to sea is something I'll never know," he said, "but if you must you must, so go ashore now in twos and mind you're back aboard here by eleven o'clock."

"We're leaving tonight then?" I asked our captain.

For an answer I got a roughish wink and was told if I had a thirst to quench I'd better be aboard quenching it. We left Lacey and Henri to watch the boat, and Bosun and I headed for the Mar Chico.

The Mar Chico was so very much the same as I'd left it that I wondered if I had been gone at all, as if the whole day with *Seac* and the MacQueens hadn't been the dreams that followed a night of too much wine. The Swiss smuggler was at the same table where I'd left him. Whether he was there still or again I had no way of knowing. Bosun and I got some wine and joined him.

"You've met the MacQueen clan, I see," said the Swiss, and what did you learn from them today?"

Bosun answered, "We've given the laddie a job with us."

The Mar Chico would be at its best after midnight and things had just started rolling when we got there, two guitars and three or four good flamenco singers. Yates was there and so was Forrest and Junior Fuller. The three of us from *Seac*, aware of our 11 o'clock departure deadline, drank with desperate speed.

When Forrest learned I'd signed on *Seac* and saw the way we were drinking, he asked me where Mac was headed.

"I don't know," I said.

"Is he pulling out tonight?"

"I have no idea," I replied.

When Forrest was out of earshot Bosun grinned and in a low voice said, "You're learnin', laddie, you're learnin'."

"Well, thank you mate," I said, "but I can tell you in confidence, Bosun, and I know you won't breathe a word, I've got it all figured out—the Italian coast and back home in ten days." That brought no response from Bosun except his same old grin.

We were back aboard *Seac* with minutes to spare and found the old man pacing the deck and looking at his watch. Two more boats were in the process of loading and I knew Mac wanted to be first out tonight, but something other than our shore leave was holding him up. Ten more minutes passed before an old Mercedes came roaring through the crowd of Arabs and braked at the sea wall, spilling out a passenger who managed somehow to catch his balance and vault to our foredeck.

As we cast off our mooring lines I was told the little Frenchman in the suit and tie with his gym bag was Robert, the "contact man," without whom our contraband couldn't move. He represented the buyers of our cigarettes, and it was up to him to see to it that they were delivered to the right parties "at the other end" where he'd go ashore with the cargo. For the trip to our rendezvous he would be considered by the rest of us as more or less part of the cargo. He said something in French to Henri and went below. The bunk under the after ladder-way was his.

Mac started the engine, backed off the sea wall, and brought the boat about in a tight arc. Out through the inner port and the bay, on our way to the Straits. My first mission as a smuggler was under way.

Seac moored in port.

CHAPTER TWO

Under the Red Duster

I thought we were on our way to the beautiful Italian coast, but the joy of it was short-lived when I realized we were heading west through the Straits and not east. For a few puzzled minutes I stood on the afterdeck and watched the lights of Tangier fall out of sight behind the bluffs of Cape Spartel. When the glow of the city was lost in the black of the sea cliffs, I went forward to the wheelhouse to talk to MacQueen. He was plotting our course on a chart and Lacey and Bosun were talking about whether to dog the watch. Since we were on our way to somewhere, I felt the rule of silence was off and risked the comment that I guessed now I'd see little of the Riviera and Portofino.

"And damned little of anyplace else either," said Mac. "If you counted on sightseeing you signed on the wrong boat. I'll not have us caught for the sake of showing you some beach resort, you can be sure of that. The less we see of land, the better off we are."

"But isn't Italy where most of the stuff goes?"

"It's the busiest place, if that's what you mean, but it's not for *Seac*. I'll tell you now that we're headed for the Bay of Biscay and a coast where this free-trader can have some room to be alone and not be bumping into every other damned boat out of Tangier."

That night I stood my first turn at the wheel, on what was left of the middle watch, and Mac stood it with me. He suspected, I think, that I had limited experience as a seaman. He briefed me on the compass and on the Rules of the Road, showed me our course on the chart, 300 degrees, almost due northwest, and marked it on a slate above the wheel. He told me what entries to make in the log and warned me of tidal races and overfalls and that the compass was known to do funny things in the area southwest of Trafalgar. He told me too that our run north would take us through sea lanes heavily travelled by merchant ships and naval vessels and to keep an eye out for them. When four o'clock came Mac took the wheel himself for the morning watch. We were abeam of Trafalgar light and *Seac* was rolling and pitching in the long Atlantic swell when I went to my bunk. My first meal on *Seac* was a tin bowl full of oatmeal and a cup of black tea stronger than I thought it was possible to make the stuff. Mac had prepared breakfast himself after his turn at the wheel. He cooked and stood watch with the rest of us. When I finished eating I took the wheel from Henri so he could eat his cold porridge.

The morning was overcast and the sea was higher than when I turned in. After Henri had eaten I watched the sea for a few minutes and went back to my bunk.

By noon the weather had worsened and we were pitching fiercely and rolling gunnels under in a broken sea. I ate very little of the sausages Lacey fried for lunch and the tea was so strong it was chewy. I was in a sweat despite the chill wind, and I didn't feel well at all.

At four o'clock we went below forward and covered the cargo with canvas against water damage, and at five we altered course from northwest to almost due north.

For a brief time we were in sight of land. Henri came to the stern while I was peeling potatoes for supper and told me the land to starboard was Cape St. Vincent. I made the mistake of looking at the land horizon across the ground swell and in short order I was on my knees feeding the fish.

Would I ever get well enough to die, I wondered, and looking at the Portuguese coast I said a quick prayer to St. Vincent. What did I have to lose? It was small consolation, but Robert, the contact man, was sicker than I was.

Despite my prayers the weather held bad the whole way up the Portuguese and Spanish coasts. We were into our fourth day and still butting our way into short head seas when Mac began to worry about making our rendezvous on time. This wasn't a storm, Mac told me, just dirty weather, but it slowed us all the same. In seas like this, we did little cooking, mainly because of the difficulty in keeping pots on the stove, and got along instead on rations of canned cheese and sardines.

When I wasn't on duty I stood a watch below in my bunk and so did the rest of them. In a bad sea your bunk was the only place on *Seac* that afforded any comfort. We rarely wore shirts or shoes at sea, and we lay in our bunks in the same trousers or shorts we worked in and swapped "war stories," some about war but most about women, or *bints* if it was Bosun telling the story. We told our stories over the rattle of the screw when the swell lifted the stern out of water and over the creaking and groaning of the boat's timbers. Noises of a small boat in a big sea.

In this weather we stuffed our crew cabin ventilators with rags and dirty laundry to keep the water out of our faces with the result that we lived in a constant haze of diesel fumes from the engine room. And despite our precautions we were still always soaking wet.

In those first days there was little to do but stand watch and get to know my shipmates. Andrew MacQueen had been a Lieutenant Commander in the Royal Navy during the last war, serving in the South East Asia Command, S.E.A.C. The end of the war found him in Singapore where he was mustered out and for a nominal amount bought a surplus MFV from the Admiralty, a boat he named after his old command. *Seac* had performed various missions in the South China Sea, including commando landings on Borneo and Sumatra. Mac sailed her back to Scotland with a crew of other former Naval types, picking up free fuel and supplies at Naval stations in the Indian Ocean, Suez, Malta, and Gib. After a couple of years he made the decision to emigrate and with his family aboard he set *Seac* on a course for Canada. Some bad luck, which he later came to regard as good luck, was the North Atlantic storm he beat into for five days before he gave up and headed to Tangier. One reason he'd left Scotland, he said, was "the bloody awful climate" and he liked what he found in Tangier just fine. Here was all the sunshine he could hope for and a good living to be made by anyone owning a boat. He was in the contraband trade in quick order. Mac kept an apartment now in Tangier with his wife, Bosun, and his teenage daughter, Jeanette. The old man would like you to think that running cigarettes meant no more to him than running a pub or some other business, but in truth none of us who sailed on *Seac* felt the excitement of being a smuggler more than MacQueen himself.

Although I had spent considerable time drinking with Bill Lacey in Tangier. I didn't know him well until we were on *Seac*. Lacey, Irish by birth and English by adoption, had been to sea in the Merchant Navy since his early teens. He was tall and lean with a longish head, and it would be hard to find anyone more opinionated, especially in matters nautical. His every statement was dogmatic enough to require a challenge. More often than not our arguments found him on one side and Bosun and me on the other. One debate that never ended had to do with the prevailing winds and currents in the Straits of Gibraltar. Lacey maintained that the current runs westerly, and his authority was one of the Horatio Hornblower books; he wasn't sure which one. Bosun said easterly, at about three knots, and his authority was the Admiralty Sailing Directions. And at sea as well as ashore Lacey had his obsession with becoming captain of his own boat. He had been Mate on *Seac* for more than a year, and his chances of rising above this station seemed dim.

Then there was Henri. This Belgian, despite his accent, spoke better English than the rest of us. He was about 35. In 1937 he was wounded in Madrid covering the Civil War as a reporter for a Belgian weekly. After Spain he completed his education at Louvain and the Sorbonne. When the Germans came, Henri worked with the underground until his luck ran sour, and he spent almost two years in Gestapo jails and concentration camps. A stubborn type, he bore the marks of numerous beatings and when he was liberated by American troops he weighed 80 pounds including scar tissue. Besides the scars, he came out of the War with a go-to-hell attitude and was set on living his life as he alone saw fit. He was still married to a woman in Paris, a fashion model, they said, and something more than beautiful, but he was doing now what made him happy, going to sea as a smuggler. Henri was the best all-around seaman and navigator on the boat. He had a sextant and shot the sun when there was one; otherwise, he helped Mac with his dead reckoning. Even before we sailed I'd heard the story of an Atlantic gale and how Henri took the tiller of a yawl for 27 hours without relief when the rest of his party was too seasick to help. It was the same storm, I think, that brought the MacQueens to Tangier. Besides being an excellent sailor, Henri was also a better than fair naturalist—our commentator on all the creatures of the sea as well as our resident historian concerning the seas and lands on our course to the north. Once he intervened in the ongoing argument on the currents in the Straits to support Bosun and explain to Lacey that the incoming easterly current to the Mediterranean was because the rivers feeding the Med gave it only about one third enough water to make up for natural evaporation. This was the kind of stuff he knew about.

I did well enough those first days and didn't miss a watch even when I was seasick, but there was one mishap. On the fourth night out, the wind came around on our quarter. Mac saw the chance to make up some lost time and rigged a sail off the foremast. I had the middle watch again and the wind, as Lacey put it, was enough to blow the stink off a man. Just before the end of my watch at four o'clock I started looking at a light somewhere off to starboard and was paying little attention to the compass and our course. Probably what I was looking at was the white and red flash of a lighthouse north of Oporto. I'd guess we were 30 degrees off course when the wind, still behind us, got on our wrong quarter and we jibed. With a loud pop—to me it sounded like a cannon—the wind carried off our sail. When Mac greeted me in the morning he had a number of choice words only a real deep-water sailor would know, but like other squalls, this one passed.

And it was that morning, our fifth at sea, that at last brought a clear day and a fresh, quick breeze. The seas were still high but in the southwest now and before noon we were abeam of Cape Finisterre and close under its granite spires. "This can be dicey here if you don't take care," Lacey told me. "To the northwest of that little rock island is what they call La Carraca, a shoal that has wrecked a lot of ships in its day."

Clear of the Cape, Mac altered course northeast to Cape Ortegal and from there into the Bay of Biscay.

When I took the wheel for my next trick, Lacey had 70 degrees chalked on the course board but told me to keep her "east northeast a quarter east."

"Stop being such a nautical hot dog," I told him.

"What's that mean, mate?"

"Grandstanding, that's what it means." He didn't understand much American but I think he got my point.

With a following sea and a friendly wind we began to pick up the time we'd lost, even without a sail. Little *Seac* seemed almost swift as she skipped down the fronts of waves in a mist of spray and foam. I was watching the cliffs of Spain recede in the distance when the rattle of a mess bowl announced our noon meal of beef and spuds. My appetite had returned and I might as well have been eating pheasant.

The fare on *Seac* was plain but adequate. Our staples were canned bully beef, potatoes boiled in sea water, bread (stale after the second day out), and tea. There was always the big pot of boiling black tea. Although we lacked refrigeration, eggs and butter kept pretty well without it. For some reason we never had fresh fruit or vegetables and when we had nothing else to complain of, we predicted scurvy. To my knowledge nobody was ever afflicted.

Someone else had cooked our lunch that day, but it was my turn to wash up. Dishwashing, done on deck, was with a kettle of hot water, some soap scraps if you could find them, and a rinse in a couple of buckets of sea water.

That afternoon I learned the terms of my employment. Mac said I would get "the regular rate" of $200 American for each run, with the option of living aboard the boat when we were in port and taking my noon meal with the MacQueens at their apartment. The benefits in port, he explained, were in return for my keeping an eye on the boat and swabbing the decks. I was going to ask about medical insurance and a retirement plan, but I still wasn't so sure about Mac's sense of humor. So much for the pay and benefits, I thought, but what happens if we're caught? I remembered what I'd heard about *Sunshine* and Henri's friend Pierre, still in an Italian jail, so I put that question to my Captain.

"Aye, there's risk enough, that's true. We'll do 2,200 miles on this run and it won't be woman's work, I'll tell you that now. You know we have no radio and what good would one do us? To get weather advisories? No matter what the damned weather we can't put into port like other boats. Whether we've got cargo aboard or not, we're marked as a contraband runner and there'd be trouble. You get into a real storm with me and you'll see boats twice our size, the fishermen and legal traders, running for port when we have to stay outside. Maybe you wonder why I asked what kind of passport you carry. Henley is a special case, but whenever I can I want to have a man with a British or American passport. It's my bloody conscience, is what it is. If they take us, I don't care Spanish, French or Italian, they'll give a break to the British or the Yanks. Take *Sunshine*. Two of them on that boat had U.K. passports and were in Malta five days after she was taken. The Frenchman Pierre and a couple of others are still in jail. No, lad, I do have a conscience. For me as owner and captain it would mean losing the boat and a year, maybe, in jail. For you and the boys it could be anywhere from a couple of weeks to a couple of months."

Mac paused to refill and relight his pipe. "Understand one thing, though. If they catch us inside their limits, all right, we'll play the game and make no fuss. But let them chase us or shoot at us when we're in international waters and there's going to be a bloody gunfight." His words made me nervous even without his bloody adjective because I had no doubt this is just what would happen. Two days earlier Bosun had opened a locker in the deck cabin and showed me three handguns, two shotguns, and an American M-1 rifle.

That evening I mentioned my conversation with Mac to Bosun and he told me a story that did little to ease my concern: "It was only three months ago. We were in the middle of the Straits coming back from Gib when a bloody E-Boat came out from the Spanish side after us. It was the middle of a Sunday morning, we didn't have a single case aboard, and we were flying our proper ensign. He circles to our port and starts crowding us to starboard, all the time hollering through a bullhorn that we were to alter course and follow him into Tarifa. My dad was at the wheel and he says, 'The bloody hell with this' and keeps his course. There was some more shouting and waving and then they start with machine gun bursts across our bow. The old man was pissed and tried to ram them. Lacey and I were laying out flat in front of the wheelhouse and the bullets came across right on top of us. Look in the morning and you'll see the hole in the galley stovepipe and a chip out of the forward mast. The Spaniard finally got the message that we weren't going to follow him to Spain and he scooted back into Tarifa. When we got back to Tangier my father called the Navy in Gib and they were supposed to have London file a protest through our embassy in Madrid, but I doubt it ever happened. The people in Gib know what our trade is, and they really don't give a shit if we get shot up or not." It was not a comforting story.

Running now to the northeast under a sunny sky, little time was spent below decks. There was always something to see. Porpoises swam along our bows until they grew impatient with our slowness and left in search of a swifter playmate. Flying fish scooted across the wave-tops, and in the morning we usually found one or two that had crash landed on our decks. Some days the sea was alive with ripples of a million sardines and other days we sailed through masses of floating seaweed dotted with glass floats lost off fishing nets.

For a few days life on *Seac* settled into a lazy pattern of steering and cooking, watching the sea and the sky, and laying out on the foredeck telling stories. Henri talked a little about his experiences in Spain during the Civil war, but had almost nothing to say about the time he spent in the lands of the Germans in the next war. Lacey had a thousand tales to tell from his years at sea in peace and war—North Atlantic convoys, strafings in the Med, St.

Elmo's fire atop the masts of a tramp steamer in the Indian Ocean. And there were stories about the French Foreign Legion garrisons at Sidi Bel Abbes and Oujda and stories about Spanish legionnaires in LaRache. Stories mostly of Spain and North Africa—gorings in the bullring, barroom fights in the joints along Gib street in La Linea, and stories about jails and prisons on both sides of the Straits. There was always plenty of talk about jails on a smuggling boat. The men who work the boats know all the best ones and all the worst ones. And there was even some talk about the ethical side of the contraband trade, the matter of smuggling guns and narcotics and carrying passengers without passports, or "bodies" as they were called. *Seac* carried cigarettes but some boats did otherwise.

Everyone agreed, or professed to agree, that running dope was a filthy business that no decent man would engage in.

"Narcotics money is blood money," Lacey pontificated. But running guns or bodies was a little different. These activities were not to be avoided on moral grounds but for the stiffer penalties if you were caught. Guns and bodies were political, with jail penalties; anything else political was . . . well, unpredictable. In all cases though, no matter what you were running, to be caught meant certain confiscation of the boat.

"In the olden days," said Bosun, "they cut a smuggler's boat into three parts, sort of a symbolic thing, I guess. Now they're too damned greedy for that. A boat is worth some money."

"Where did you learn that, about cutting up the boat?" I asked.

"From George, who else."

"Has *Seac* ever carried anything except cigarettes?" I asked him.

"Once, but never drugs or guns. Once we carried two Jews from Tangier to France. They got so seasick we thought at least one of them would die before we got them ashore. After that it was back to strictly cigarettes."

Chapter Three

Rendezvous

On our sixth night out of Tangier the atmosphere on *Seac* changed. We all remembered the purpose of the trip north, and a crew that a few hours earlier was into story telling and sunbathing was now all business.

We were approaching the rendezvous. In the next 24 hours I would learn what smuggling was all about. As we cut across the Bay that night we were blacked out even to our running lights and ran to the east under less than a quarter moon, a smuggler's moon. There was little talk and voices were kept low. Again I had the middle watch, "the graveyard watch," Lacey called it.

When I took the wheel at midnight I had my introduction to the cooked log. Until then I had seen only one log, the book in which we entered our position, course and wind, and sea conditions. Now I saw a second logbook in the wheelhouse with entries for all the watches of our six days at sea, but quite different. It showed that for six days we had run on a course dead north from a point off Lisbon and were now in the North Atlantic at 49°40′ N Latitude, 08°30′ W Longitude, 150 miles west of England's Land's End. I turned back to the page for the first day of the voyage and found that our destination was Cork, Ireland.

Folded in the log was a cargo manifest, countersigned by Tangier's Port Captain, also for Cork.

At dawn I noticed that the Red Duster had been struck. Not only were we running without lights, but we were sailing without a flag. With our top speed of eight knots it was Mac's hope to stay unnoticed as long as possible as we neared the territorial waters of France. We kept our easterly course through the day and an hour after sunset we made our landfall on the French coast south of the Gironde Estuary and north of Arcachon Basin. The five-second white flashes of Hourtin light were dead on our bow. Our point of rendezvous, arranged three weeks before we sailed by coded cablegrams between Tangier and Bordeaux, was plotted on our chart, but any hope of contact had to wait until morning.

Mac reduced speed, and we stood off to the south and "stoodged" in a circle through the night, without lights and as quietly as possible. Our Irish log now showed we had strayed from our course and were halted for repairs somewhere west of the Isles of Scilly.

At dawn Mac and Lacey surveyed the coast through glasses and took cross bearings on landmarks. To the south at 45°08′ N Latitude was the lighthouse at Hourtin and northward, near the mouth of the Gironde River at 45°29′ N Latitude, the burned-out hull of an American Liberty ship.

Seac was where she should be, at the third point of a triangle with the light and the wreck, about ten miles off the coast. We were on the rendezvous. Here, if things worked out, we would be met by a fishing boat that would take our cigarettes and slip back into its home cove sometime after dark. I took the glasses myself and got a closer look at France, a stretch of yellow dunes behind a white line of surf. The *South Biscay Pilot* had it right when it said "recognizable or conspicuous objects are few and far between" on this coast.

We stayed on station and sailed north and south with Henri lying on the roof of the wheelhouse with the glasses. The morning passed and so did most of the afternoon. Nothing. As the hours went by our skipper paced the deck without letup. "A thousand bloody miles we've come and they can't come out ten miles to meet us when they should." Mac cursed our customers, a degenerative lot who "had the bloody cheek to call themselves smugglers."

The sun was beginning to set and supper was forgotten. Mac ranted on about the fuel he was using and the risk of our being spotted from one of the lighthouses. Even if we were taken for a foreign fishing boat poaching in French waters, we'd be investigated. Mac talked now about turning around and going home, but this was for the benefit of Robert, to whom Henri supplied a translation. As if our contact man could do anything about it. He had looked at the chart, looked at the points on the coast, and decided that this was in fact the rendezvous.

Now Mac talked about putting Robert ashore—a standard MacQueen ploy, I was told, intended to scare hell out of the contact man. The people who sailed in this capacity almost always were landsmen, not seamen, and rarely knew how to swim. Mac had Robert sweating. "We have that old rubber raft in the paint locker. We could give him 'til morning to reach his people and get them out here. Translate, Henley."

"But Skipper," Lacey said on cue, "that raft has a leak in it and would be good in the surf for about 10 minutes at best."

"Translate that for the man, too, Henley." It was all a charade, I knew, but the idea of a night landing did seem exciting.

It was just about then that we sighted a boat. We watched her grow larger in the dusk as she came right at us until we could see the bone in her teeth. We strained to make out her size and shape. Was she our boat or an armed patrol? Mac kept our stern to the oncoming boat and his hand on the throttle, ready to go. He had something new too, a .45 automatic tucked in the waistband of his shorts. All the excitement of sea smuggling was crowded now into the next three or four minutes. When those unreasonably long minutes had passed, a stained once-white oysterman pulled alongside and the grinning faces of three *contrabandiers* peered over our gunnel.

Then it was a confusion of heaving and sweating and swearing. We dismantled the saloon skylight and as Bosun and Henri pushed the cases up to us, Lacey and I hefted them across to the Frenchmen. The two boats rode side to side in the heaving groundswell and squeezed the water up in spouts that rose above the wheelhouse roof and fell to drench us all. Loose cases toppled with the rolling of the boats and twice fell into the sea to be retrieved with boat hooks and more swearing.

Despite the bedlam, the hold of the smaller boat was filled and the pile of cases grew higher on her deck. The Frenchmen pleaded that they had taken aboard as much as they could safely carry and said they'd return the next night for the rest. The pilot of the oysterman was a tall aristocratic looking bird and there were tears in his eyes as he vainly tried to stop the cases being tossed onto his boat.

"Only thirty more," Henri called in French when he really had seventy. "Keep 'em moving."

Before we off-loaded our first case, Mac was handed a brown paper bag, and he was still in the wheelhouse counting out piles of French and American bills when the last of the cargo was out of *Seac.* We helped Robert over the rail, and he waved goodbye sitting on the precarious pyramid of cigarette cases as the small boat prepared to cast off. But before they let go their lines, the Frenchmen fulfilled a custom of the trade and handed us two large baskets filled with bottles of wine, fresh fruit, eggs and bread. It was dark now and in a very few minutes the white boat was out of sight. We pulled the corks on a couple of bottles of wine and cooled ourselves in the rising wind. We were happy the job was done, no one more so than Mac. He smiled for the first time since we left Tangier. "Drink up, Laddie," he said to me, "you're a smuggler now."

The trip back across the Bay was pleasant and relaxed. The weather held good, and we went about washing and mending our clothes and peeling spuds for the next meal. Lacey even got a torn sail out and worked on it with his broad needle and twine, wearing his sail-maker palms.

Maybe once a day Mac or Bosun gave the engine a squirt of oil and sometime each day one of us went below to empty the old soup can that hung on the diesel to catch drips. We rarely had to wash our deck as the freeboard was low enough so the sea did the job for us. When we'd eaten most of the fresh food we'd gotten at the rendezvous we hailed a fishing boat out of Santander and threw them a carton of cigarettes. In exchange the fishermen almost maimed us with the number of bonita they tossed aboard *Seac*. We fried a couple in canned butter for a feast to remember.

Seac was a pleasant enough boat to sail in, but it did have a couple of shortcomings. For one, getting a drink of water or a kettleful for tea was a major adventure. Our only tap was in the unused forward galley, which was crammed with old mattresses and other crap even after the saloon had been emptied of cargo. Down the ladder in the dark, trying to find the light-switch on the overhead beam, shift a dozen or so stored articles and you were on your way to getting a cup of lukewarm water. And when you got it, you needed one hand to cover the cup until you got back on deck. This was to keep out the roaches.

Customs patrols and storms were always a concern, but not a constant concern like the cockroaches. The little buggers trooped about the boat like they owned it. There were more roaches in the hold than cigarettes and more roaches in the spud locker than potatoes. By the hundredfold. They were in our blankets and between the pages of the books we read. When we slept they were in our hair and in our ears. I learned early on that when you felt that tickle you shook your head and never, never stuck your finger in your ear. No one could say for sure when or where they had first come aboard, whether they were Malayan, Scottish or Moroccan roaches, but they seemed to be with *Seac* to stay. They laughed at ordinary bug sprays and ate DDT for breakfast. We had to live with them and they had to live with us. Anyway, they were better than rats and *Seac* had no rats.

Personal grooming on *Seac* was haphazard at best. When we were on a run no one ever shaved and usually we washed our hands and faces from a bucket of sea water. Except for Bath Day. When it was required, and our schedule and weather permitted, Mac would point the boat into the wind, idle the engine and spend 20 minutes or so pumping our bilges. It was then, by Captain's orders, that all of us except the Captain himself stripped and went over the side for a bath with salt-water soap. Sometimes we even had a quick game of follow-the-leader, diving off the bow and off the roof of the wheelhouse.

It was late in the afternoon the day after our rendezvous, and we were having our bath party when Mac spotted a whale lying about 100 yards off. The creature blew a spout into the air just like any old picture-book whale you ever saw, and our leader called us back aboard *Seac.* We scrambled out of the water soaking wet and naked as the whale. Our leader was excited, jumped the old diesel up to top speed, and closed rapidly on his prey to investigate. As we drew near, the huge monster gave us what we swore was a dirty look, went head down and flukes up, and disappeared into the briny deep, leaving us feeling a bit foolish and guilty for having annoyed her or him.

The whale encounter was a onetime thing and our bath parties were just a couple of times a trip, but the poker game, once we'd made our rendezvous, went on every day, good weather and bad. No matter what, the game had priority. Often the wheel was lashed and we sailed with no one in the wheelhouse except for a compass check after every four or five hands. Poker on *Seac* was a serious and wild affair. Our stakes were pesetas and no one ever knew, 'til we got home and checked the exchange rate, how much of our pay in American dollars we might have lost. The poker itself was pretty bizarre, if it was really poker at all. We played everything from a good tight hand of five-card stud to the old man's favorite, Southern Cross, a game that took a *high* five-of-a-kind to even be in contention. I didn't care much for this game, probably because I had more than one royal flush lose to some other guy's royal flush that was ruled "more natural" than mine, whatever the hell that meant.

The evening following our encounter with the whale we had company of a different kind. At sunset we had Cape Ortegal in sight off our port bow when a flotilla of warships loomed out of the coastal haze from the southeast and came at us in two files.

"My God," said Bosun, "it's the bloody Spanish Armada."

"They do appear to have us outgunned," said Lacey as they got closer. "Talk about more force than is necessary, this is bloody absurd." There must have been ten or twelve ships, destroyers, destroyer escorts, and what looked to be a heavy cruiser. All of them were gray, but their number markings seemed to be in different styles. We couldn't see their flags.

As they closed on us Mac's opinion was that they weren't Spanish at all. "They're not even all from the same navy," he said. "My guess is what we're looking at is some kind of exercise of that new alliance business, what they're calling the North Atlantic Treaty Organization." Whatever they were, they weren't after *Seac*. The two columns closed up, passed us a mile astern, and disappeared north into the dusk.

We were around the corner and running south, somewhere off Vigo Bay, when our engine quit. "Walter," as Mac called our old diesel, had been balky since the night we off-loaded, but now at three in the morning it stopped dead. In a matter of seconds everybody was awake and on deck. The sudden silence, as Mac put it, "was like a bloody thunderclap."

We drifted 'til dawn, then all morning and into the early afternoon. MacQueen was in the engine room trying everything he knew but without much luck. He had the engine going in fits and starts but couldn't keep it going for long. Finally he came on deck and announced he was going to do something he said he would never do—put into port. "We'll be at risk, but at least the only cigarettes we have aboard is what's left of the ship's case and those might even be useful." He meant that the ship's case was a case of cigarettes put aboard each boat in addition to the regular cargo and were for the crew to smoke or barter as they saw fit. It was cigarettes from this lot that got us our bonita.

We turned east and on two cylinders limped into the fishing village of Bayona. As we came into the harbor past the headland and ruins of a castle, Mac ran up our quarantine flag. With the prospect of shore leave we shaved our whiskers, scrubbed ourselves with sea water, and put on the cleanest shirts each of us could find.

Bayona was a beautiful little fishing village that would compare favorably with the best small ports on the Italian Riviera and the Côte d'Azure. We dropped anchor among the local fishing boats and waited for clearance to go ashore. Mac went below again to work on the engine, but the rest of us eyed the cafés along the waterfront with growing impatience.

"Gawd lu'me," said Lacey, "I've seen coves like this before. All they do is fish and fuck and this time of the year they don't do much fishing."

We waited for the authorities to come but there was no sign of them. They must have known we were there, everyone else in the port did.

Lacey was wrong about one thing, this time of the year they did fish. It was coming on sunset and we watched the Spanish trawlers glide in and out of the harbor and marveled at the size of their crews. Some of them must have carried 100 men and boys, every one of them grinning and waving as they passed us.

One crowd was particularly raucous and gave us a "Hello, sailor boys" in English that sounded a bit derisive. The man at the wheel was apparently caught up in the fun and the next minute he ran his bow into the stern of a boat in front of him. It was our turn and Bosun, in his best Scot bellow, gave them our own "Hello, sailor boys."

Right after this a rowboat brought us our representatives of the Spanish Government. The boat itself was old and battered and looked like it might sink under its load. A lad of ten or eleven pulled the oars and carried two *Guardias Civiles* in their gray-green wool uniforms and their patent leather hats. Each held a rifle and looked very important indeed. When they boarded *Seac,* Mac was on deck to greet them and although they told the boy to stay where he was he paid no attention and climbed aboard himself. After much handshaking Mac filled out three or four forms to the satisfaction of the constabulary and allowed them to examine our log, the one he chose to show them, and our manifest to Cork. He offered them a drink and both downed a generous portion of whiskey. They were considering refills when, in a voice as big as a peseta, their oarsman was heard from, "Whiskey, *señor, por favor.*"

He was too young for whiskey, he was told by the Guards, and he answered that maybe he was too young also to be rowing two grown men about the harbor on such a warm evening. With a nod from one of the Guards, Mac filled a glass for the boy who with solemn formality raised it in toast: "*Salud y pesetas y fuerza....*"

"*Bastante, nino.*" Enough, his elders admonished him and watched him down his drink in a single gulp. All smiles now, the trio got back in their boat and wished us welcome to the town. Before they cast off, Mac gave each of them a carton of cigarettes.

"Don't for a minute think they don't know what we're up to," said the old man. "They know what we are and more than likely have a damn good idea of where we've been. And for sure they know what port we're bound for when we leave here."

Our friends the *Guardias* put another boy to watch our dinghy when we tied it to the seawall and Lacey went off on his own to hunt up a lady. The rest of us got a warm welcome from the locals in one of the cafés, and found it hard, with all the hospitality, to even buy a drink. Only twice that night did I hear the word *contrabandista* and it was said in a friendly fashion, perhaps even with admiration. We returned to *Seac* full of good food, good wine and good feeling. Mac finished his repairs in the morning and after a quick swim in the icy water of the harbor, much colder than the water in Biscay, we were under way again.

With 600 more miles to sail there was still time for another mishap. The loss of the sail on the trip north had been my fault and so was what happened now to our drinking water. Other than handling cargo one of the few jobs at sea that would raise a sweat was the chore of hand pumping fuel oil from our reserve tanks to the main tank, and the same with our fresh water. Each job had to be done a couple of times a trip and Mac told me to pump some water after we left Bayonne. I got one of the pair of hand pumps from the paint locker and was working for maybe ten minutes when I realized my error. Too late. I had put the last of our fresh water through the pump we used for the diesel oil. The water was now unfit to drink, of course, and we had to get along for the next four days on a triple strength brew of oily tea. With good cause I caught a lot of unkind words and nasty looks from my shipmates, but it was Mac who put his thoughts to music. His composition went to the tune of *Let Me Call you Sweetheart* and he had all of us, even me, singing it for the rest of the run:

"Let me call you Captain,
Let me sail with you
Up to the Bay of Biscay,
Up to the Rendezvous.

You can pay me in dollars
of the U.S.A.
And I'll be sick and useless
all the bloody way."

Sixteen nights after we set out from Tangier we were back home. A few minutes after midnight we dropped our anchor off the stern and tied up between the *Wilson* and the *Djombie*. Mac handed me a roll of $200 American, and in less than an hour we were washed, shaved, and ashore on the town.

John Moore with bonita in hand.

John on *Seac* with telescope in hand.

Chapter Four

Ramadan

The Mar Chico was our last stop before we left and was our first stop when we got back. With Lacey, Bosun, and Henri I sat down to a meal of tripe with plenty of red wine and fresh bread. A dwarf off one of the Spanish boats danced to the flamenco guitar and added a Medieval touch to the old place. Afterward, we moved to the Aduana, met Hans and Yates, and then on to Dean's. We were greeted warmly by Dean and by Priest, Nancy, and Forrest. They said it was good to see us back but nobody asked where we'd been.

Everybody stood a round of drinks, and then more rounds, and we were given all the news. Bud Priest told us Pierre was still in jail, and that *Sayon* was still laid up in Spain. He'd been over to Algeciras on the ferry and spent two days and nights drinking with his crew in the bar of the Hotel Reina Cristina. "A morale builder," he called it. Also he told us of the French film crew that was in the port making a movie about smugglers and getting in everybody's way.

From Nancy we heard that while we were gone Priest punched out the Cultural Attaché to the American Legation one night at Parade and exchanged some punches with one of his own crew another night—or was it the same night?—at Johnnie's Bar in the rue Foucauld. Dean told us the *Sonning* had been taken off the Italian coast, and that *Porcupine* was somewhat luckier. The Italians had gotten her cargo of 832 cases as it was being put ashore, but the boat and her crew managed to escape and run back to Tangier.

It was late when we left Dean's and we stood in front for a few minutes to watch a Berber donkey train on its way from the hills to the Soco Grande. The street was full of Arabs now, all night long. Ramadan, the Moslem month of daytime fasting, had begun and the night was for eating and drinking.

Bosun left us and headed for the MacQueen apartment, but Lacey and Henri and I had some coffee in the Soco Chico and made our way to Freddie's place in the walls of the Casbah. Freddie's was a night club of sorts, had a dance band and hostesses, and advertised itself as "the world's best place for the world's worst people."

While the Spanish bars nearer the port were patronized by the men off the boats, fishermen and smugglers mostly, who were satisfied with cheap food and cheap wine—and on occasion cheap women—cheap Freddie's catered to the more expensive tastes of a different crowd: Tangier's pimps, hustlers, and genuine thieves. You could get champagne in Freddie's and almost anything else if you had the money. We drank beer. We drank and danced with the girls and were ready to call it quits as the morning sky started to brighten when Henri had the idea to cap our homecoming by watching the sun come up from the top of the Casbah. We made our way through the alleys that became passageways and passageways that became steps—all of them smelling of hashish and urine—up to the little plaza that overlooks the old city, the Bay of Tangier, and the Straits of Gibraltar. It was empty now;

too late an hour for the usual story tellers and snake charmers. From here the new Tangier of apartment houses and hotels was mostly out of sight—only old Tangier on the Barbary Coast with all its ageless smells and noises. As we stood there we heard the report and echoing rumble of the cannon that signaled the beginning of another day of Ramadan and listened to the muezzin from the minaret in the Soco calling the faithful to pray. We could also hear the counterpoint of the dance band at Freddie's, still at it, calling others to play.

Henri went back to living on Pierre's little sailboat with Pierre's wife, Bosun stayed with his family in the apartment, and Lacey and I were living on *Seac* until the next run. By noon we were on our feet again, made some tea, and gave the decks a quick wash. On most mornings we would be joined on the boat by Mac and Bosun for a couple of hours work, but not today. At one o'clock we climbed up the hill to Mac's apartment to have the lunch that was part of our deal.

The MacQueen apartment was at 9 rue Velasquez, on the fourth floor of a building with no elevator. Sid Paley and Elliot Forrest had an apartment next door at No. 7, and so did Bud Priest. Mrs. MacQueen put out a decent meal, which I had maybe two or three times a week. Short on meat and long on potatoes but nothing to complain about. The main reason I didn't eat there more often was the long hike up the hill and the long climb up three flights of stairs.

After we ate we stopped at the British Post Office and there, waiting for Lacey, was Mr. White's reply from France. That Lacey actually got an answer to his letter at all was a surprise, but White's response was a bigger surprise. He agreed to Lacey's proposal: no changes, no conditions, no strings. *Antonina*, he said, needed some work but would be ready to be picked up in Villefranche in five weeks. Captain Lacey had his command!

The rest of the afternoon amounted to what passed in Tangier for a business meeting, five of us assembled at our table outside the Puerta Café. The syndicate Lacey had in mind was himself as director and captain, By Yates, Hans the Dane, and me. One more man was added. Bob Gates, at Yates' urging, was sent for and joined us. How he fit into the picture with Yates, however, had puzzled me since Nancy's dinner party. Most of the time By seemed anxious to avoid his company or even discuss him, but now he wanted Gates to be a partner and sail with us, and Lacey agreed to it.

Lacey talked and planned non-stop for hours, only pausing to gulp his beer. He offered me the mate's berth, probably because of my American passport, and without waiting for an answer he made Hans our engineer. "We'll be on a run in eight weeks time," he said. "By will manage things ashore while we're out and he can line up cargoes. Even if we can't buy a cargo right away I know a Spaniard who'll let us carry 400 cases he's got coming in. We can make a run with every moon and we can even make money carrying stuff that's legal. There's lots of cargo to be moved to the Canaries." Although we probably had about the right number in our group, one man as general shore agent and four of us at sea, some other names were kicked around and there was mention of Elliot Forrest who was known to have connections in Italy and France as well as in Casablanca and Tangier.

"We'll steer clear of him, thank you," said Lacey. "That lad has some funny ideas—dangerous ideas. At home we'd call him a wide boy. There's trouble there we don't want and don't need." He didn't elaborate.

In the weeks that followed, my activities and attention were divided between *Seac* and the plans for *Antonina*. I spent the mornings working on *Seac*, at least when Mac and Bosun were aboard. Mac would go below and work on the engine, Bosun did the odd job of carpentry and Lacey and I scrubbed, chipped, and painted. As the junior crew member it fell to me one morning to be hoisted up the foremast in a rickety bosun's chair, on what looked to be a worn and frayed line, to paint the mast top and cross tree. No fun at all.

When we weren't working ourselves, we watched them on the *Wilson* tied up alongside of us. *Wilson* was an old wreck of a fishing boat out of Tarifa across the Straits. We never learned where she got her unlikely name, unless it was in Gib. There wasn't a plank or beam in her that didn't have some rot, and an old Arab stayed aboard at night pumping until dawn to keep her off the bottom.

Each morning a crowd of Spaniards of all ages arrived and swarmed all over her with hammers, saws, and bottles of wine. We couldn't see what they were getting done but all the activity left Lacey and me tired just watching them. They were a friendly bunch though and shared their wine. And although *Wilson* looked like it had been blown into Tangier on the last *levanter*, two nights a month she limped over to the Port Captain's office and took on 40 cases of cigarettes. Then she'd be gone for four or five hours and make a transfer somewhere out in the Straits. *Wilson* was a short-order smuggler.

Wilson was on our starboard and *Djombie* on our port side. *Djombie* was an MFV like *Seac* and was under the command of a Latvian exile named Serge, a very big man with shaggy black hair, maybe as big as Bosun and me together. He and another seaman had sailed to North Africa from Riga in a converted life boat, getting along on what food they could grub from passing ships. Serge had the reputation of being a first-class skipper and a holy terror ashore. He was well known to Tangier's bar proprietors and not unknown to the Tangier police and the town's pawnbrokers. On a good day—or maybe on a bad night—his gold watch could be in and out of hock two or three times. One evening as he was getting ready to go ashore we watched him pin his watch and a gold fountain pen under a shoulder pad in the old jacket he wore. "I hope," he said, "that when my money runs out I won't remember where they are."

I spent my afternoons and almost every night with the *Antonina* group. Lacey had acquired an old M.G. and Yates owned a Chevy convertible. In twos and threes, and sometime all five of us, we started looking for a house to rent. Captain Lacey felt that this was needed to provide us with a headquarters and lodgings suitable to our new station in life.

In a matter of hours, after hearing from White, Lacey was laying plans for a business empire, a multi-national conglomerate that would have offices in Gib, the Canaries, and Casablanca and would be funded by the enormous profits he expected from our operation of *Antonina*. He selected various locations near the Place de France where we would soon have a laundry, a store, even a restaurant. Whole afternoons were spent in the Marshan district and up on the Mountain inspecting available villas and discussing our servant requirements. Rather too quickly, I think, we all began to succumb to Lacey's fantasies. In addition to cigarette runs and trips to the Canary Islands Lacey proposed we carry pilgrims to Mecca and also accommodate some ex-Nazis in Tangier who were looking for private and discreet transportation to South America. The last idea got no support from the rest of us, but we let Lacey have his dreams.

Our rides around the International Zone weren't limited to house hunting and corporate planning. We swam at Robinson's Beach on the Atlantic, drank in a nifty little bar on Cape Malabata, and drove out to Cape Spartel and the Cave of Hercules. The cave is a special place. Under a limestone headland called Ras Ashagar—the bald head—the Atlantic comes boiling up inside and fills the place with sea spray. A tribe of gnome-like Moors still cut millstones in the cave as they had from time beyond memory. Once, and perhaps still, the site of pagan rites, the cave was a landing place in the 1920s for guns for the rebel chief Abd el-Krim and in the 1940s a mule stable for the Spanish Foreign Legion.

It was a rare day we didn't have a drink at Dean's, and it became a ritual to stand in his doorway on Fridays and watch the Sultan's Horse Guard with their drums and horns go down the hill to the mosque behind the Soco. Not only did Tangier have three Sabbaths in every week but the city observed close to 200 secular and religious holidays a year. If banks and stores weren't closed for a Jewish holy day they were closed to celebrate a saint's day, a French military victory or a Spanish or British naval battle.

After dark we gave our trade to the Spanish bars and the more upscale Melodie's, Djory's, and Johnnie's, and sometimes even the Parade. We liked Johnnie's because it was run by a Polish American and was the only place in Tangier you could get a Budweiser.

It became apparent that *Seac* needed a number of mechanical repairs and would be in port for awhile, probably missing a run at the next new moon. She did make one trip when Mac took her over to Gib for fuel oil and to buy canned goods and whiskey, and we had a good two-day outing. We tied up at the South Mole, got our shore passes at the Police station in Irishtown, had a quick drink at the Rock Hotel, and then Lacey and Bosun acquainted me with the pubs up above Camp Bay. It was a break from the *Antonina* business too, as Lacey didn't discuss his plans in front of the MacQueens. While the three of us drank ale and ate bangers and meat pies, Mac was off meeting with someone to discuss business, but he didn't say with whom.

On the way back across the Straits I heard Mac say something to Bosun about flying to Naples, and I really wondered then who he was doing business with, and who I was actually working for.

I spent most of my evenings after our Gib vacation at either Dean's or the Parade, sometimes alone, sometimes with the *Antonina* gang. Lacey was already spending our expected profits. When we weren't in a corner planning, we drank with pretty lively company, including Capote, Bill Bird, Paul Bowles, and Eugenia Bankhead. Eugenia was even more animated, she said, than her sister Tallulah, and with pretty much a free-form lifestyle. She told us about her "special friend" and benefactor, a lady member of the DuPont family in Wilmington with whom she had some sort of ambiguous sexual relationship. Bowles spoke of his recently published novel *The Sheltering Sky,* and Capote, drunk almost always, and flushed for months now with the critical success of his *Other Voices, Other Rooms*, lisped on more about his lady friends than his boyfriends: Gertrude Stein had said this to him; Barbara Hutton, whom he most often referred to as Mrs. Cary Grant, had done such and such to him; and on it went.

One night, late, I was drinking alone at Parade and had just taken on yet another ration of George's lore of the old-time smugglers, Cruel Coppinger, the Carters of Prussia Cove, and assorted other of his "rascals," when Paul Bowles came in and ordered a glass of juice. Bowles wasn't a drinker but was getting into *kif* and *majoun* pretty good. We got talking about how he came to Tangier.

"I came here first on Gertrude Stein's recommendation," he said. "In 1931 in Paris she took to calling me Freddy, after my middle name, and she said 'Freddy, you and Aaron Copland must go to Tangier, its a place where the sun shines every day.' So we came. I came back to stay in 1947." (As it turned out Bowles had come to Tangier the same way I had, on a Norwegian Fern Line freighter out of Red Hook, Brooklyn, bound for Casablanca, generally an eleven-day voyage.) "In forty-seven I had Gore Vidal and Cecil Beaton here for a while, but I was the only one to make this town my home."

Some nights I left Parade or Dean's with the feeling I was the only guy in Tangier who had never had dinner in Gertrude Stein's apartment.

On another night the same week, Miss Stein's friend Bill Bird fell to reminiscing about Hemingway. In 1922 the two of them had taken a hiking trip in the Black Forest. "In the afternoon we stumbled on what was obviously a military exercise, a clear violation of the Versailles Treaty. That night Hem and I both wrote stories for our papers. Hem was with the *Toronto Star* then. When we were done we read each other's stuff. Hem took his own dispatch and tore it up. He said, 'Bill, after seeing what you wrote I can't put this crap of mine on the wire.' The point gentlemen, and I assure you the story is true, is that one night many years ago Bill Bird out-wrote Ernest Hemingway."

He paused, finished his drink, and went on: "When I think of the good times and the bad times I had with that son of a bitch, lots of years ago now. The fiesta in Pamplona in 1924, we were there with our wives, Sally and Hadley, and with Dos Passos. It was my first time and Hem's second year at the fair. He got in the ring and waved a cape at bulls all right but every one of them had their horns padded, did you know that? His only chance of getting hurt was if he was stepped on. But no, to be fair, I've seen the bastard bleed. In 1922 we shared a hotel room in Genoa covering the International Economic Conference when a hot water boiler blew up and it took me an hour with a dozen towels to mop the blood off Hemingway and off the walls and floor. Some guy he was in those days."

On another occasion shortly thereafter, he asked me, "Did you ever meet Tom Archibald? He lives on the Mountain." I said I hadn't met him. "Well," Bird said, "it kind of makes the point about not being so far removed from the past. The Battle of Trafalgar was in 1805, an event we think about in terms of history books. Tom is about 80 now, but in 1892 or '93, thereabouts, he met an old Arab here in the city who as a boy sat on Cape Spartel and watched the Battle of Trafalgar, or at least saw the ships and the smoke and heard the guns. You have Tom tell you about this and you'll think it was he who saw the battle."

The Parade and Dean's were where you talked literature. The Mar Chico and the bars around the Port were where you talked bullfights and heard all about the great ones—Belmonte, Joselito, and Manolete. But that was for other nights.

For a number of mornings Mac had us work a little harder and a little longer to get *Seac* cleaned up and painted, all "ship shape and Bristol fashion," as he put it. He hoped to complete the work before he and Bosun flew to Italy.

On two mornings we had visitors, three in all. An American named Teague came aboard with a proposition that Mac run 300 M-1 rifles to some Basque insurgents in Santander. Teague had the guns and the customers but he needed a boat. Mac turned him down, saying after he left that Teague really didn't have to be doing such stuff. He was probably right. Teague was Barbara Hutton's current "closest friend" and in a few weeks, when Hutton left Tangier, he would be driving the newest and biggest American automobile in town, bigger even than Paley's.

The next morning I finally got to meet Charlie Miranda whom I kept hearing about. Charlie was supposed to be from Chicago but looked and talked like he was out of New York's Mulberry Bend. He was middle aged, overweight and overdressed to be climbing around boats. Charlie was never without a tie and jacket, and he wore enough rings and bracelets to take him to the bottom if he ever fell overboard. There were stories about Charlie. He was said to be "connected" and "a money man for the Organization." Once, they said, he killed a man. He looked the part.

He and Mac retired to the deck cabin for about an hour, and it was one of the few times, other than at sea, that the door was closed. Later that day at Dean's the word was that Charlie was just back from one of his frequent trips to Naples where he had stayed at the Hotel Turistico, a favorite place, I learned, with Tangier businessmen and quite by coincidence the sometimes residence of Lucky Luciano.

Our third visitor arrived shortly after Miranda left. His name was Bradford and he was on the staff of the British Consulate. He said he wanted to talk to all of us, looking at Lacey when he said it. "We have information at the Consulate," he said, "that Mr. White has offered to make his boat *Antonina* available to Mr. Lacey." I looked at Mac who showed no surprise at the news.

"The *Antonina*," he continued, "as I'm sure you all know, is a boat with a very bad history and a very bad name. The last time she was in Tangier, a year ago, she was impounded and Interpol's narcotics people tore her apart, literally tore her apart. It took two weeks of repairs before she could go to sea again. She's gotten the same treatment in Italy and Gib. When White was in Gib with her, he was followed by police and Interpol agents every step he took ashore. They had teams on him around the clock. Her reputation, gentlemen, is no better now than it was then, and I am here as a representative of the British Government to warn you, Mr. Lacey, and anyone else who may think of becoming involved, that you had all best keep clear of her."

He left without saying anything more and without comment from any of us. After he was gone Mac took me aside and said, "I know all about *Antonina* and Lacey's deal and I'll say the same thing Bradford said, keep away from it. He talked about Interpol and they're tough. I'll guarantee you, that as new to this business as you are, Interpol already has a dossier on you. I'd love to see mine; I hear from a friendly sort at the Consulate that it's two inches thick, but then, maybe I'm just boasting. Anyway, take my advice and forget *Antonina*. You have a berth aboard *Seac* as long as you stay out of trouble."

That was one of the days I went up to Mac's flat for my noon meal. After lunch the two of us sat talking for a while, while Mac fiddled with a Luger Henri had bought for him in Casablanca, a weapon he usually kept on the boat. His wife glared at him when she saw it. His life as a contraband runner was to be left behind him in the port; he was not to bring his work home with him. This included talking in the apartment about cargoes or runs. But on this day he broke all the rules. He oiled his gun and worked the slide as he talked. "I'll say it again, give serious thought to what Bradford said about *Antonina* and joining Lacey. You're a grown man and free to do as you like but you'll have to decide between *Seac* and the other boat. And another thing, is Elliot Forrest involved in this?" I said he wasn't. "Steer clear of that man. He told me only a couple of days ago that I was daft to pay for my cargoes. He said there were plenty of cargoes just to be grabbed and plenty of boats too for that matter. It's a serious crime your countryman is talking. I told him I didn't want to hear about it." And with that the gun went off.

Mac never said later, "I didn't know it was loaded," but I'm sure he didn't know. Luckily it was pointed down and the bullet only ruined a rug on its way through the floor. We had a brief discussion about possibly going down to the apartment below to see if there were any casualties, but Mac decided against it. When his wife calmed herself and was ready to have her say, I guessed she'd have a lot to say and I left. There was one casualty and one funeral from the gun accident. The MacQueens had a small dog and a little cat. The loud shot in the small apartment drove the dog bonkers, and he ate the cat, at least enough of her to make her dead. The next morning Mac brought the pussycat's mortal remains aboard *Seac* in a brown paper bag and had me weight the bag with rocks and row out into the outer harbor and give her a proper sea burial.

The accident with the Luger was the starting gun for the accelerated events that overtook all of us involved with *Seac* and *Antonina,* and the things that happened took place in the charged atmosphere of the last days of Ramadan when tension in the city was increasing with each day and night. The month of fasting would end on the first night that the next new moon was visible; before the fasting ended, however, frayed tempers would lead to violence. Twice in a week Arabs were pushed to their deaths off roofs in the Casbah, and all day long the little white ambulances clanged through the streets. The Casbah and the Soco were to be avoided now, at least until after dark when people were eating. It had been our habit, until recently, to have our nine-cent lunch once or twice a week, but we quit this for a reason that had nothing to do with Ramadan. The café's gourmand menu featured *lapin* almost to the exclusion of other meat dishes, and one day as we made our exit through the Casbah and were kicking alley cats out of our path someone speculated as to where the place got all those rabbits they fed us at such a reasonable price. This was our moment of revelation and we found other places to eat.

As Ramadan ground to a conclusion we spent more time in the Spanish bars near the port, especially the Mar Chico. One night we fell in with a French police sergeant on leave from Port Lyautey in the French zone, where I used to have a drink with him occasionally, and a Welshman who was formerly with the British police force in Palestine. The two of them grinned as they compared their respective methods of applying electricity to recalcitrant Arabs standing in tubs of water.

It was more pleasant to talk with Paul Bowles who came into the place about two in the morning. He was working now on a new book he planned to call *Let it Come Down*. "It's starting out, at least, here in Tangier," he told me. "I don't know if this place will be in it but I found a little whorehouse bar in the Medina that I'm sure I'll use." He did and called it the Bar Lucifer.

One morning Mac announced this was the day he and Bosun were going to Naples. "A business trip," he said, "to get a few things straightened out." Mac left me with instructions to help Henri get *Seac*'s hull scraped and scrubbed in his absence. I was about to ask why Bill Lacey wasn't going to be in charge of the job when he told me: "I've fired Lacey. I asked him which it was to be, *Seac* or *Antonina*, and it seems he's going with White's drug boat. So be it. Bosun's my mate now. And I know Lacey's been talking to you about the Fairmile. I'll not press you now, lad, but I want to know where you stand. I've got to organize my next crew and I want to make a run as soon as I get back so I don't lose the new moon. Think it over and we'll talk next week." I was glad he didn't want my answer right away because I knew I still wasn't sure about the *Antonina* venture.

They left on a noon flight for Rome and, after I saw them off, rather than join Lacey and Yates for more planning and plotting, I went to Dean's alone. Dean was another one on Mac's list "to steer clear of" as the old man was convinced Dean was a paid informer, selling sailing information to the Italians and Spanish for a piece of the confiscated cargoes. I didn't believe this, but even if I did I would have gone to Dean's anyway as it was too good a scene to miss. That afternoon Dean was directing everyone to the new item on the bar's bulletin board. It seems that for a week or more a jealous rival for Miss Hutton's affections had been spreading the friendly little rumor that her friend Teague had syphilis. When Dean opened at noon, Teague was waiting for him, asked for a thumbtack, and posted the results of his negative Wasserman test. He was gone when I got there, but the report stayed on the board for weeks and I'm sure was brought to Barbara's attention. Dean ran his place in his own style.

That afternoon someone told him his hair was a little too long in back, and for a minute or two the critic got some hard looks from the rest of us for fear Dean would close early. Instead, to our relief, he made a call, a barber came in, and bar service was suspended just long enough for Dean to set up a chair in the middle of the room and get his haircut. That was in the afternoon.

After supper I got back to the bar a few minutes after the evening opening to find Dean in a state of agitation.

His single employee was an Arab who swept and mopped the place in the morning and otherwise cleaned up spills, washed glasses, and squeezed lemons. Dean had him for years, and he was more dependable than anyone had a right to expect in a place like Tangier. But not tonight. Instead of his dark-skinned citified Arab in his European clothes and greasy red fez, enter his apparent stand-in, or perhaps successor: an ancient fair-skinned Berber with light brown hair that stood out electrically and wearing a burnoose that was nothing but patch upon patch. Above his bare feet his shins were wrapped in burlap. He showed what was either a grin or a grimace, we didn't know which. His teeth were white and regular where the Arab's had been awful—"a disorganized mouth," Nancy had called it. He stood at the end of the bar waiting for an assignment, but Dean found that, while he had been able to communicate with his Arab in French, this fellow spoke only a Berber dialect, perhaps even the old Shilha. In any case, a language nobody here knew. This was one problem and maybe Dean had a problem too with the fact his new man had a skin color lighter than his own.

"This is preposterous," Dean ranted, "my boy Mohammed was here all afternoon and never said a word. Now see what I get. What is it I get, I don't know. Is there someone here can show this creature how to squeeze a lemon or wash a glass? He followed me in when I opened the door and he just stands there with that bloody silly grin. Now honestly, doesn't he look like a wild man? I want him away from here before he frightens off all my trade, but who can make him understand? For God's sake, he may be deaf for all we know." Dean screamed at the man, first in Arabic and then in English, Spanish, and

French, but to no avail. He thrust a handful of pesetas at him, probably more than he paid Mohammed in a month, and pointed to the door. The man neither accepted the money nor moved to leave, but instead went behind the bar, grabbed a towel, and started washing glasses. Evidently he had some instructions before he arrived. For a while Dean was speechless, an unheard of thing, and just watched him. But there was a pretty good cadre of clients now and everyone had something to say.

"Did he come on a camel? Has anybody looked outside?" asked Nancy.

"He's not from the desert," Bud Priest said. "He's not a Tuareg, I know that crowd. He's a Berber from the mountains, maybe the High Atlas, but more likely the Rif Country. Better we should look for his donkey, not his camel."

"Don't stand too close," Nancy said to Dean, "he hasn't eaten all day."

"Ah, but just look at him," said George, "and think of the stories he could tell us. He's a piece of African history is what he is. He's of an age to have fought with Abd el-Krim in '21 and I'll wager he did." All of us, even Dean, looked at the old warrior with interest as George retold the story of the Rif rebellion, the tribesmen's rout of the Spanish and their years of hill country war with the French. It was as good as a slide show, but only for one night.

Noon the next day Mohammed was back and it was the end of the Berber's cameo appearance at Dean's. But one other thing happened that night that I'd shortly have cause to remember. Dean, in repeating some bit of gossip, referred several times to Mr. Yates, but it was clear from his story that he was speaking of the sailor Bob Gates and not By Yates, our shipchandler friend. It reminded me of something similar at Nancy's party at the Cecil but I couldn't think why there'd be any confusion despite the similarity in their names.

The next morning, after my holiday at Dean's, I met Lacey and Yates at the Puerta Café to find that our syndicate was missing a partner. "Hans is gone," By told me. "You saw the Dutch freighter that went out this morning early? Hans was on it and so was a good part of the cash receipts from my office. How he got it I don't know, but the money's gone. It looks like we have a four-man company now."

"That should be enough," Lacey said, "at least to pick up the boat." That was in the morning that we had four men. By noon our band was down to three. Like the decampment of Hans, I missed it. I had *Seac* to myself now since the fired Lacey had moved ashore to a hotel, and I was aboard taking a midday nap when two armed marines from the Legation and a couple of local police arrested Bob Gates in the Mar Chico.

In addition to Tangier's multiple postal services, the city also had four separate legal systems. Moslems were under the authority of a Koranic court, Jews a Rabinical court, and all others a mixed court except for Americans, who were under the jurisdiction of the U.S. Consular Court operating out of the Legation.

When I got back to the shipchandler's office and heard the news, Yates was dripping sweat and his color wasn't good. He told me about Gates, the whole story:

"His papers don't say he's Gates, they say he's Byron Yates and that's my name and they're my papers. His real name is Larkin and he's a rat and a bastard. Oh, he's an American all right—he deserted the Fifth Army in Italy and that's where I met him and I damn the day it happened. When the war ended he was managing a nightclub in Portofino, and I was purser on a Liberty ship. We got to know each other pretty well and he told me he was a deserter. There was a law in Italy then that gave him some protection. The Army knew who he was and where he was but couldn't arrest him. At the same time he was fed up with Italy and was going crazy when his old company commander started hanging around his club every night, sitting and watching him. It might as well have been Mark Clark. He wanted in the worst way to leave the place, but had no passport and no papers, nothing. There was something about a girl too, but I'm not sure what. He asked me to help him with papers but I wouldn't do it. Then when I left Italy I found my purser's ticket and other papers were missing, all but my passport. I came here and forgot Larkin—for awhile. I'm here three months and who shows up. All the port towns in the world and he picks Tangier. And he comes here as By Yates. We talked and came to an understanding that he would stay and keep my papers, I didn't really need them anymore, but he would call himself by another name. He became Bob Gates, at least when he was sober and remembered the name, but sometimes he was Yates. And now he's been arrested and my own ass is in all kinds of hot water with the Legation." [I learned later that they held Bob Gates, or Larkin, a few days in the Malabata jail in Tangier and then moved him to the brig at the U.S. Naval Air Station at Port Lyautey, a brig I helped build a year earlier. Eventually he was court-martialed in the States and sent to Leavenworth.]

It was four days before the new moon; everyone was getting their boats in shape for a run, and Henri and I planned to clean *Seac*'s bottom the night that would bring the spring tide. This would make careening the boat against the seawall that much easier. Then that night the *levanter* came barreling out of the east. When the wind came up, the boat crews hurried down the hill from the bars and put out extra lines and extra anchors. The boats that were lying outside in the bay, *Jessbee*, *Donna Beta,* and the Fairmile *Whitechapel*, all moved in to the protection of the inner port. For the next two days and nights the men stood by their lines or went over to help out on other boats that got themselves in trouble. When the wind finally slacked off a bit most of the men went back to the bars. A *levanter* was bad at any time but worse when the moon was right to start a run.

All day and all night port-bound Spanish seamen sat playing dominoes in the Puerta del Sol and the Aduana, and all the bars in the city were filled. "The Black Cat," the town's classiest bordello, did a month's business in three days. Captains and crewmen looked out on the port from the doorways of Freddie's and the Mar Chico waiting for the wind to stop. And finally it did stop, early in the morning before the night of the new moon.

Ramadan was about to be over; other boats loaded and left port; and Henri and I started our cleaning job, a project we expected to be uneventful. We warped *Seac* over to the seawall by the port warehouse and tied her fast.

When the tide ran out to dead low water, the boat's keel rested on the bottom and she leaned over against the wall. The four Arabs we'd hired stood knee deep in the mud and went to work scraping the barnacles and crud off the hull. Late in the afternoon the starboard side was done and at six we floated her on the incoming tide, turned her around, and went up to the Aduana to wait for the tide to ebb; then I think we decided to go to the Puerta del Sol and maybe even Freddie's for a short visit. When we returned it was midnight, the tide was again at dead low and *Seac* sat on her keel. To our pleasant surprise our gang of natives had gone back to work on their own and were just finishing cleaning on the port side. We paid them off and Henri pulled the cork from a bottle of wine. With our wine we left the cabin to survey the scene of our accomplishment and as we both stepped onto the deck it happened—the damned boat fell away from the seawall and flat on its side. At first it felt like she was rolling to port in a heavy swell but she kept on going. We both grabbed at the cabin doorway to keep from going into the mud and water and the noise was awful—all the sounds of disaster. First there was the bang of the mooring lines all snapping at once, then there was the creaking and groaning of the boat's timbers and the godawful roaring crash of everything that was loose, or was breaking loose, smashing about and going overboard. Our mouths hung open as we watched the flying paint buckets, pots of jam, and fuel oil drums. When it was over *Seac* lay on her side in the mud with her port gunnel under water. We climbed atop the starboard side of the cabin, now its roof, for a post mortem. It became clear that when the tide ran out the second time *Seac* never leaned back against the seawall as she was supposed to, and as a result, I guess, of our two or three drinks ashore we never noticed it. Our combined weight on the port-side deck was just enough to start her going.

With some shouting we reassembled three of our boys and had them salvage what they could from the water. *Seac* was not a pretty sight. When she went, two heavy fuel oil drums from the starboard deck forward shot across to the port side and took with them the entire skylight structure over the forward galley. And then we both realized the real problem. Worse than the damage was the fact that the tide had turned and was beginning to inch up toward the open hatchways and ventilators.

The tide was rising, the boat was not. I made my way forward to the paint locker and got a hand pump and Henri got one of our Arabs back aboard. We lowered him into the engine room with instructions to keep pumping until further orders. Then we agreed it was in God's hands: His and the Arab's in the hold. The incoming tide would either float her or sink her, and it would be too much for any man's nerves to stay around to see which way it went.

We climbed ashore and headed up the hill. We paused at the Mar Chico, but decided it was too close to the port and instead stopped in at an Arab café in the Medina, probably drawn to its open doorway by the music of an oud. The room was maybe forty-feet square with benches and tables along the walls. No alcohol but mint tea in glasses and we ordered a couple.

Paul Bowles, with a pipe in hand, nodded from across the room but I wasn't sure if it was a greeting or just a *kif* nod. The three of us were the only non-arabs in the place, the only men not wearing the *djellaba*. When our tea was served the man on my left passed me a pipe. Being a non-smoker I passed with a muttered, "Merci," and gave the pipe to Henri who took a puff or two of the hashish. Henri and one of the Arabs exchanged a few words in French and Henri asked me if I wanted some *majoun*. It could be gotten right away, he said, but I told him no, what I really needed was a drink.

We finished our tea and went on up through the Soco to Dean's. The place was empty when we got there, and Dean probably would have also been closed except for the music he was listening to. After hearing our story, he recognized that we needed some more alcohol for medicinal reasons. He had Lisbon on the radio and they were playing the *Scheherazade Suite*. After giving us drinks, Dean was lost again in his reveries of Pavlova and Nijinsky, Covent Garden, Vienna and Paris, the ballet troops, and the opera companies. As the symphony neared its climax Dean relived a ballet—or maybe it was an opera—he remembered from Monte Carlo forty years before. When Radio Lisbon signed off for the night Dean was on the floor of his barroom in a death scene, paring knife in hand and his eyes rolled back in his head. He even made us forget *Seac* for a little while. It was nearly light when we left Dean, had a final drink at Mar Chico for courage, and went back to the port. There, thanks be to God and our Arab, we found *Seac* floating. We put her back in her berth next to the *Wilson* and drank the only bottle of wine we found unbroken.

In the full light of morning the mess on *Seac* was disheartening. Henri had stayed aboard and together we went ashore to get some coffee and fried dough sticks—anything to delay a real damage survey and the cleanup job. When we did return to *Seac* and started putting things in order, we weren't at it long when Mac and Bosun hove into sight, having returned earlier than expected from Naples. Henri and I had a hurried confab and since it was the right thing to do, we told Mac the truth: "We were ashore, Skipper, no more than five minutes, maybe ten at most, and the goddamned Arabs must have fooled with our lines and dumped her. If we hadn't both pumped all night 'til our arms were about to fall off she'd be on the bottom now." The language that came out of Mac's mouth was dreadful. I tried to follow the best I could but he used at least four words I'd never even heard before. I thought maybe they were colloquial to North Scotland but Bosun later said no, he'd never heard them before either. For the rest of that day and the next we all worked to get *Seac* back in shape and ready to sail. Mac cleaned and tuned the engine, and Bosun built a wooden hatch in front of the wheelhouse where the demolished skylight had been.

When it got dark and I was washing up to go ashore, Mac told me he'd made a deal in Italy for a new and larger boat, and he asked me again whether I planned to sail in *Seac* or in *Antonina*. I'd given this a lot of thought in the past week, and I kept thinking back to what the man from the British Consulate had to say. I told Mac I would sail in *Seac*, reasoning that there was enough excitement in just running contraband without getting my ass in a jam with something really dangerous. I found Lacey and Yates at Dean's and told them what I'd decided. They were disappointed but we were still friends and they bought me a drink. Lacey still planned to fly to Nice to pick up his boat, and he and Yates discussed who they might get to fill out their depleted crew. Lacey saw Yates glance at

Elliot Forrest, who was at the far end of the bar in a whispered conference with Charlie Miranda, and shook his head no. "Mac says he's a bloody pirate and I think he's probably right."

Yates suggested Junior Fuller. "He just might do," said Lacey, "if he's willing to quit all the programs he's supposed to have going with O'Brien." In addition to illegally selling cars in Spain the two of them were said to have a deal going to smuggle Swiss watches into England and were possibly involved in an enterprise for the transport of raw alcohol to Greece. None of these ventures could have been too real or too great, however, because later that night Fuller accepted Lacey's job offer.

The next day Lacey and Fuller left Tangier on a flight to France with a middle-aged Irish drifter they picked up in the Mar Chico. (In France, we heard, Lacey was able to hire a Frenchman to complete his crew.)

MacQueen was very anxious to get going himself. "I can't afford to miss another moon and another run," he said. As far as the Old Man was concerned our new crew was all set. He had taken on an Australian named Tony Townsend, and with Bosun, Henri, and me there were five of us. Then, on the same day that Lacey and his people left for France, the long lost Pierre, late of the *Sunshine*, resurfaced in Tangier after six months in an Italian jail. After a brief but no doubt exciting reunion with his wife (Henri prudently stayed aboard *Seac*), he surprised Mac by asking for a berth on the coming run. He would be an extra hand but Mac signed him on: "With six of us I'll make no money but we can have a man at the helm and still have a decent poker game."

Pierre Coupay, as I'd heard, had once been a medical doctor in France, giving up his profession for reasons that were never asked about. He was a good looking blonde guy in his thirties, even tempered and knowledgeable about any number of things. In short a good man to ship with.

Townsend was also a good shipmate but another breed of cat. Probably about the same age as Pierre, he'd led a different sort of life. To say he was tough is to say Einstein was bright. By his own account, and no one doubted him for a minute, he left Sydney as a teenager after he kicked an off-duty constable to death in a pub brawl. He had a dozen scars and a story for each one: a ricochet bullet in Bombay in '36, a piece of bomb fragment in Malta in '41, and so on. But Mac hadn't hired him because he needed a storyteller. Tony Townsend was a first-rate ship's engineer, as good as there was with small boat engines, and *Seac*'s old Kelvin was starting to need more and more attention.

The order of the day now, and every day, was to work like hell to restore our boat to seaworthiness and for all of us "to keep our bloody traps shut" about when and where we were going. Since his return from Italy, MacQueen was obsessed with security. "It's all set now," he said, "the coast of Biscay belongs to *Seac* and I'm damned if we let anybody find us out. Just keep buttoned up and all of you stay out of Dean's and the Parade, its only a matter of days now before we go. And steer clear of the legation and consulate people." Keeping our plans secret a little while longer shouldn't be all that hard, I thought, we had done alright 'til now.

But then it was Captain Goldy who came rowing over from his sailboat and came aboard with a smarmy look that told Mac he was not there to make him happy. "Old Bluebeard" Mac called him, and his white chin whiskers twitched as he delivered his bad tidings. "Andrew, my friend, they know where you go, they know where you're taking your stuff. By tonight every bloody informer in the Soco will be trying to sell the information if they've not done it already. A terrible thing, Andrew, but I'm glad I got you before you left on another run. Aye, you'd have found your rendezvous as full of customs boats as fleas on a dog. It's a good job I heard them talking, a good job indeed."

"My thanks to you, Goldy," said MacQueen without expression, "and where do they say I go?"

"How they found out, Andrew, I don't know but the word is out that you're making runs to Cork and unloading off the Irish coast." Bosun and I watched Mac's face for his reaction and we weren't disappointed.

"The bloody clots!" he roared—one of several of his expressions that I found pretty funny—and pounded the side of the deck cabin with his fist. "Damn the lot of that Judas crowd," he stormed. "Hear what he says, lads, and steer clear of the Soco and Dean's and the types you find there. Now we have to make new plans, find a new buyer and probably lose two or three runs, one at the very least."

"Shit oh dear, this is bloody awful." Mac treated Goldy to a quick whiskey, was profuse in his thanks, and couldn't wait 'til he was back in his dinghy to have a good laugh and get on with his preparations. Mac decided then that it was only proper that he continue to sign off on the

Port Captain's papers and carry a manifest for Cork. Our security was still intact. For awhile, anyway.

After Goldy left, Mac and the others went ashore for various reasons and I was alone on *Seac* when Serge came aboard. A few weeks earlier Martin had sold his *Great Scot* to Caulfield from Gib and the big Latvian had been hired away from *Djombie* to be her Captain. Now he was ready to take the boat out but couldn't locate certain charts. I knew we had a second set of old charts in the wheelhouse and without giving it a thought I let Serge take them. He was hardly gone when I realized that the Atlantic charts I'd given him not only had our course to Biscay plotted on them but had a couple of rendezvous sites marked as well. Could our security be breached any worse than this? As long as Mac didn't know.

The plan was to leave just before dawn the next day. That night Bosun and I, true to form, found ourselves at Dean's despite its being on our captain's "steer clear" list. By midnight we were in no pain whatsoever and I had stopped fretting about my gaffe with the charts. There were Brits and Colonials all over the place and with Bosun I raised my glass to "Home Rule for Scotland" and "Cast off the English Tyrant's Yoke," not much appreciated by George and the other Englishmen present. Our ultimate revelry though was in song, a thundering rendition of Mac's ditty that had become *Seac*'s alma mater and fight song:

"Let me call you Captain,
Let me sail with you.
Up to the Bay of Biscay,
Up to the rendezvous."

We woke up, Bosun and I, but not before we were into the chorus for the third time. The people no doubt wondered why we shut up, paid up, and left for the boat so fast.

By four in the morning our full crew was aboard, we had 300 cases loaded, and we laid at anchor waiting for the flood tide and our contact man.

Before we cast off from the loading wall I saw Mac huddled with Charlie Miranda next to the Port Captain's office. Charlie seemed to be everywhere.

A little before five o'clock an Arab sculled alongside with a passenger and in the light of his lantern I got my first look at Louis, our contact man, someone I'd get to know pretty well. He was one of the smallest men of adult age I'd ever seen. His black hair was plastered to his head and hc had a black shadow across his jowl no matter how often he shaved. But like Robert he was dapper. He wore a dark double-breasted suit with the lapels turned in against the night air. "Just tuppence short of a bob," said Mac, surveying our last bit of cargo. Louis gave us a "bonjour," and when he went below we saw he carried a small suitcase and a shoebox tied with string that had a tired lettuce leaf sticking out under the lid. "Well," I said to Henri, "it looks like the reputation of our galley has finally gotten out. This one has brought along his own rations." With that we hauled anchor and Mac started the engine.

Chapter Five

The Honest Thieves

That night, when we sailed out of Tangier, I didn't know what might be in store for me or whether I'd made the right decision in opting for *Seac* over *Antonina*. What I did know was that we'd probably have some bad weather ahead of us, weather that started a week earlier and 4,000 miles away. A tropical storm, born near Puerto Rico, had regenerated 700 miles east of Florida and before we left we had reports from Gibraltar that it was causing havoc with shipping in the western Atlantic. The last news we heard was of the Danish freighter *Paris* in trouble off Hatteras and that the storm, now hurricane force, was headed toward Nova Scotia. As we moved north the storm was expected to turn east across the Atlantic, but without a radio we had no further word of its progress.

From the beginning, even before we were out of sight of Africa and the light on Spartel, there was a different atmosphere on *Seac*; there was certainly less joking around. This was the first run in a long time that Mac was sailing without Lacey, and this might have had something to do with it. But mostly it was probably the weather. Even in the Straits we were butting through short seas and a strong wind and seemed to be making no progress at all. Two days of lousy weather and we were only off Cape St. Vincent and closer to the coast than Mac liked. And then in the span of two hours the wind dropped, the sea calmed, and we were in fog.

A storm at sea can bring fear to a boat but the onslaught of wind and water at the same time gives men strength and keeps them too busy to worry much. Fog brings a different kind of fear, the fear of helplessness. In the first hour the broken front of the fog bank was like drifting streamers of smoke and then it closed around us until the sky and the sea and the fog were one seamless mass. The black clouds we had at the start of the run were gone and at noon the silver disk of the sun hung by our aftermast. We ghosted through the wall of whiteness at just enough speed to maintain steerage way. Mac kept the wheel and studied the chart and the pilot book, *Spanish Coast Pilot*, which reminded him, he said, of the local fishing boats often at anchor in the deep water south of St. Vincent. The rest of us huddled together in the bow and listened to the whisper of water along the side and the voices of fog-horns off in the distance.

We were too close to land and at the same time too close to the fishing grounds and the main shipping lanes. Somewhere to starboard lay the mass of rock that was Cape St. Vincent, so full of sea caves that the Pilot book noted that "the noise of the sea breaking in them can be heard at some distance." But on this day the sea was almost flat.

Cape Sagres, just across Beliche Bay, was a jut of limestone the ancients said was the end of the world. Henri told us this and he told us about St. Vincent, the Sacred Mount occupied by the gods; it was once unlawful to set foot on the Cape after dark. Prince Henry the Navigator died at Vila do Infante, near Sagres, on land granted him by the crown. "The cape of gods and goats," Henri called it and it was not too far away beyond the grey curtain. In the fog it was hard not to think of John Masefield's line, "Yonder's Cape St. Vincent and the Dead."

Every muffled sound we heard increased our anxiety. Two more things that *Seac* did without were a horn and a bell. "We should be making some noise," said Henri, "to let people know we're here."

"We could holler," said Townsend.

"Or sing maybe," said Pierre, an idea that had some appeal. Bosun's suggestion of the "Dead March" from Handel's *Saul* was rejected; no one knew the words—if there were in fact words. We settled for a few choruses of "Lilly Marlene" and, at Tony's demand, "Waltzing Matilda." We were off key but loud, and who knows, maybe it worked. No ship ran us down.

The fog persisted through the night and we saw neither the red flash of Sagres light nor the white flash from the lighthouse on St. Vincent attached to the old convent at its summit. The *Pilot* said "fog signal" on Sagres and "sirens" on St. Vincent, but we were never sure we heard either one. In the morning the fog began to lift and the white envelope parted to show the sea and the sky again.

For a couple of days the weather was only moderately bad. The wind was up, the seas were high, and we sailed without sun under a mackerel sky. We'd seen worse weather, and would again, but we were happy to be out of the fog.

It was about then that Tony Townsend took over as cook. We had rotated the cooking job, the same as wheel watches, and one day Tony complained about the food he was getting. It was our third straight meal of *Seac* stew, the bad weather house specialty: ten pounds of spuds boiled in sea water, three or four cans of bully beef, and a dozen onions. And a half bottle of ketchup when we had it. We tied the pot on the stove with a length of line and let it cook for half a day. Anyway, Tony complained and Mac asked him if he could do better. Yes, he could, he said and he took over as full-time cook. Not only did he do better, he turned out to be a cooking fool. Some afternoons, when we still had eggs left, he prepared a soufflé as we sat with him in the deck cabin listening to his stories of his pub fights and his women, his sheilas. He gave the pots and pans the same care and attention he gave Walter, our engine. Every night the big Aussie surprised us with a new delicacy. If his soufflés were good his meat puddings were great. He steamed his puddings in a cotton cloth and they only lost a bit of their popularity when we discovered the cloth was one of his own well-worn T-shirts. The very personal touch of a master chef. Pierre, being a Frenchman, was our recognized food critic and said even a meat pudding cooked in a dirty undershirt was better than spaghetti.

"You don't like spaghetti?" someone asked him. "You eat spaghetti," he replied, "with warm water for sauce, three times a day for 168 days in an Italian jail and then tell me how much *you* like spaghetti."

And on the subject of food, we found out what was in the little box our contact man had brought aboard, the one with the lettuce leaf hanging out. It was the second day after the fog lifted. We noticed Louis had a worried look and was poking around the boat like he'd lost something. He didn't answer Pierre when he asked him what he was looking for, only showed him the empty shoebox.

We found out what it was when Tony went below after supper and discovered a large African snapping turtle crawling under his bunk. It was a gift for his nephew in Bordeaux, Louis told us, but Tony saw to it that it would swim the last 700 miles if it was ever to get there.

We were just past the Burling Islands, maybe 60 miles north of Lisbon, when the weather closed in on us with a vengeance. When I went to my bunk that night there was just enough roll to put me to sleep. At midnight when Henri woke me for my watch there were seas falling on our after deck and the wind gusts were blowing rain. Even before I was on deck I was soaking wet. At the top of the ladder I held onto the door frame and tried to see something in the dark. The sea was confused and turbulent and you couldn't tell where the waves were coming from. All our decks were awash and we were shipping it cold and green. No moon, no stars, and no clouds to be seen; just blackness. I pulled myself forward on the life line rigged along the deck-cabin bulkhead and took the wheel while Henri made his log entries.

"Heavy weather," he said. "The course is there on the slate but keep her a couple of points more west so her nose is into it. Don't let the wind take her around too far and you'll be alright." He closed the book, turned off the overhead lamp and closed the wheelhouse door behind him. The only light now was from the compass binnacle.

On a calm night there was a wonderful peace standing alone in the wheelhouse with your thoughts back home or a thousand other places, but in a storm it took two hands on the wheel, your mind on your course and your eyes on the compass card and the sea ahead. *Seac*'s steering was all manual with twin cables running from the wheel back along the deck to the rudder. In a broken sea like this one it took strength to hold a course and keep her into the wind, but it was hard enough to keep standing on your feet. By three o'clock the wind had backed to the southwest and the following sea piled more water on us and made steering that much tougher. When the sea lifted our stem, the rudder was out of the water and the wheel swung loose in your hands for an eternity before she answered the helm. Four o'clock was a long time coming. At the end of my watch, I checked the barometer, found the glass low and still falling, and made my log entries. I lashed the wheel with a piece of line and groped my way back through the wet to wake up Bosun. I found our crew cabin stuffy with diesel fumes after the wind and spray on deck. I shook Bosun enough to be sure he was awake and had one foot on the cabin deck before I went back to the wheelhouse. The trip was bad enough, and I didn't want to do it again. The compass indicated we'd lost a bit off our course, but I put it right by the time Bosun showed.

Bosun came into the wheelhouse with a large can of fruit he brought with him from Tangier—as a personal item, he made it clear. On a boat that until recently was feeding us only *Seac* stew, canned fruit was a real treat and I was pleased to see he had two spoons. A portion of the fruit bought Bosun a half hour of my company.

When the weather was as bad as this, no one got much sleep although most of our time off watch was spent in our bunks. The result was a marathon bull session that ran around the clock and lasted for days, with Pierre smoking his Casa Sports and Tony his Camels out of the boat's cargo. Pierre told us how *Sunshine* was chased, machine-gunned, and finally forced to heave to, luckily enough with only one crewman nicked with either a bullet fragment or a splinter from the disintegrating boat. He never said much about his experience as a doctor except to tell us it was good, for medical reasons, for a man to get roaring drunk every so often, to give a good shock to his system and all his organs.

Bosun, on the other hand, had no great stories to tell, but he loved to sing and he loved to recite. He had a little book of chanties and sea poems and whenever the sea was really knocking us about and the engine fumes and cigarette smoke had us all groggy, he'd recite his favorite, something called "The Sailor's Consolation." It began:

"One night came on a hurricane,
The sea was mountains rolling,
When Barney Buntline turned his quid,
And said to Billy Bowling:

"A strong nor'wester's blowing, Bill;
Hark! don't you hear it roar, now?
Lord help 'em, how I pities all
Unhappy folks on shore now!"

The rest of the piece was a lament for the poor landsmen who had to endure falling trees and toppling chimneys and such. We enjoyed the recitation but somehow the poem fell short of making me glad to be at sea.

The weather stayed miserable past Vigo Bay and to Finisterre and beyond. It was our fifth day at sea, I think, when our steering gear fouled. By the time Mac had us all on deck, *Seac* was already swinging with the wind and taking monster seas aboard on the weather side. The problem was a steering cable jammed in a pulley on the after deck and an immediate grease job was called for. The boat was in clear danger, but Bosun rose to the occasion. He was into the deck cabin and reappeared with an open pound-can of butter. With Tony hanging on to his ankles and me hanging on to Tony, Bosun half crawled and half swam aft and buttered up the cable and pulley. When we pulled him back through the wash, he was near drowned but the wheel was working again and Mac was putting us back on course.

First with the fog and now with this storm, we were all paying closer attention to the charts and the pilot books. We finally got to Finisterre and the chart carried the caution that this coast "should be given a wide berth in thick weather." We did just that and turned the corner, and on past Cape Ortegal we were now into the Bay and into the teeth of what Mac, Henri, and Tony all confirmed was a full gale with a force ten wind on the Beaufort Scale. And it blew like this all the way to the rendezvous, sometimes out of the north and sometimes out of the west—sometimes with us, and sometimes against us. There wasn't a move *Seac* didn't show us. She rolled and pitched and lurched and did corkscrew twists into the waves with water spouting from her scuppers. To a man we were wet, tired, and miserable. Cooking was suspended, even the *Seac* stew, and when we ate at all it was canned cheese, sardines, and soggy stale bread or canned biscuits. The wind squalls whipped us with a spray like white smoke and piled the sea ahead of us into black mountains of water. These were seas that put fear into every man aboard, and there were times when my own breathing stopped dead.

For a few seconds we'd hang suspended on the crest of a roller and then pitch down its slope until our bow was buried in the hollow of the sea. Each time there wasn't one of us who would have bet a bottle of Stork beer that we'd ever come up again. Crossing the Bay all but one of our jerrycans of paraffin were carried away and the fear of going overboard ourselves was on everyone's mind. We were already a day late and all but hove to in the storm. The sea changed hour by hour but never for the better. At times the wind was so strong it tore the tops off the waves and for a little while flattened the sea like a lake—a short lived and treacherous lake. Then without warning we were faced again with a running wall of water, and when we hit it pieces of the sea reached our mast head. But despite it all we reached the rendezvous.

MacQueen made his landfall north of Arcachon on the eighth day. We steamed north and were on the rendezvous at twilight and then stood off through the night with our bow west into the storm. It was still blowing and raining and the Bay was all scud and spray and tumbling seas. There was no comfort on *Seac,* but this was weather welcomed by the smuggler for a rendezvous. It limited the activities of the patrol boats and caused the coast watchers to relax their vigil. For us, though, it was either ride it out or be wrecked. "In heavy storms," the *South Biscay Pilot* told us, "this coast offers no safe shelter." Every few months we heard in Tangier of boats being lost at sea. Recently the *Mary Angela*, owned by Scott and Caulfield in Gib, was wrecked on the rocks near Casablanca.

In the morning there was no sign of any patrol boat, nor was there any sign of our contact boat. *Seac*, it seemed, had the Bay of Biscay to herself. We waited all day and whoever was in the wheelhouse kept glasses on the coast both north and south.

By afternoon it was still raining but the wind had slacked off a bit. It would take more than a change in the weather to cheer our skipper. He was on the rendezvous with no contact and after the long tough run north he had no extra fuel for stoodging around. His mood was darker than our St. Vincent fogbank. At dusk I looked at my watch and gave Mac until seven o'clock to tell Louis he was putting him ashore. At five past seven Mac called us all together and with Henri translating he said that Louis would have to be put on the beach during the night and get some people out to us in the morning or we would start home for Africa.

I'd heard the routine before, but tonight there was a different tone in the old man's voice and a very serious look on his face. I realized he really meant it this time and Louis knew it too. Louis was as concerned as MacQueen about the rendezvous. He was responsible for the delivery, and he made it known through Henri that he would do anything in his power, almost anything, to get the stuff ashore. It would go hard with him if the cargo went back to Tangier.

"Surely, *mon Capitaine* will understand and wait one more day. Surely my friends will find us tonight and if not tonight then most surely in the morning. *Certainement.*"

"I'll wait not a bloody minute more unless I know something is being done ashore to get these bastards off their asses and out here to do business," Mac argued with all his Celtic charm. "Tell him he either swims in or we're on our way home with his bloody cigarettes. No more waiting."

"He says he can't swim, Mac," Henri told us. Like Robert, Louis was a landsman, not a seaman. "He wants to know if we can't put him ashore in the dinghy."

"Not bloody likely, that," grunted Mac. "There's nothing but big surf on the beach from the Gironde to Arcachon, and I'm damned well not riding the little bugger into a port. No, he either swims in, and tonight, or we're done here." The discussion continued: You must swim, I can't swim—we were getting nowhere. But I had an idea of my own. The little Frenchman had to get ashore but couldn't do it on his own. But maybe with some help. I went back to the wheelhouse and looked again at the chart and pilot book.

"Listen, Mac," I said, "What if I swim in with him. I put him on the beach and then I come on back. It shouldn't be hard to do. It's a sandy beach, no rocks, and probably too remote to have much in the way of coast watchers. We could both wear life jackets and I'd see to it the little guy doesn't drown."

MacQueen's first reaction was predictable, "You're daft, Yank." But when he thought about it he began to see a way to save the run and his profits. "We could maybe do what you say. Move in towards the beach after dark as far as it's safe to go and then carry you and the Frenchman in the dinghy in close to the surf. You both go bathing; he's ashore and on his way to a telephone; and you're back to the dinghy and back to *Seac*. We'll figure out some light signals or something. Could work, could work."

We had some cold Spam for supper and when it was completely dark we headed inshore at about three knots. A groundswell from the west pushed us along. There was no rain but a solid mass of black clouds made the night dark enough to hide what we were doing. We sailed slowly, blacked out even to the light in the compass binnacle. At eleven o'clock Henri in the bow heard the first rumblings of surf. Mac brought the engine down to dead slow and Bosun began to take soundings. He threw his hand lead line maybe a dozen times before he found a bottom. At a mile offshore we had seven fathoms. When Mac reckoned we were within a half mile of the beach and the line showed three fathoms, he idled the engine and told us to get the dinghy off the cabin roof and into the water. With the engine noise cut you could hear the surf clearly now. We put the dinghy over the stern.

In the time it took us to come inshore the west wind had freshened and carried the chill of early Autumn. I counted on the water being warmer than the air as we made preparations for our landing party. Someone found a disintegrating set of oilskins in the chain locker and Louis, stripped to his shorts, used them to wrap up his shoes and suit. We tied the bundle to the Frenchman's waist and someone found two cork life jackets, one for Louis and one for me. The two of us got into the dinghy with Bosun, who took the oars. Mac agreed to show a light signal after 30 minutes and then to repeat it at ten-minute intervals until we got back to *Seac* in the dinghy. Mac said that while we were gone he'd see if Tony couldn't cook some pancakes for us, provided his flour wasn't wet and he had enough paraffin left in the stove. We cast off the dinghy's painter and the wind and the swell carried us in toward the beach. By the time Bosun had his oars in the water *Seac* was out of sight.

Bosun rowed in the direction of the roaring surf, and in a few minutes he decided he was in as close to the breakers as he dared go. Now he had to shout for me to hear him. "Are you going in with your clothes on?" he asked.

"Give me some credit, will you buddy," I said. "I'll get goddamn pneumonia if I ride back to *Seac* in wet clothes in this wind. You keep my stuff nice and dry for me."

When we went into the water, which was warm enough, Louis had on his drawers and I had on nothing except for my life jacket. I let the little guy clamp onto my shoulders and I started to swim to France. For a few minutes it went alright, but only for a few minutes. I had just taken a couple of choppy little strokes to pull us to the top of a swell when the whole Bay of Biscay and most of the Atlantic Ocean fell on top of us. I wish I had seen that wave—it must have been something. The next 90 seconds were bursting and curling and exploding so fast there wasn't even time for panic. Hanging upside down in the boiling sea, the two of us scudded along together until one of the thundering breakers loosened Louis' hold on me and he disappeared in a confusion of foam, his white face spouting sea water like a plaster garden decoration. A hundred yards more of ass-over-teakettle somersaults and then, finally, sand under my feet. And there was Louis, bobbing face down not 20 feet from me, his clothes bundle still attached. If the son-of-a-bitch is dead, I thought, the mission's a failure. I got to him, got his face out of the water, and dragged both of us through the undertow and up on the beach. I put him on his belly and watched him slowly open his eyes and start to breathe again. He made noises like a bathtub draining. He was alive, at least a little bit. I sat there next to him for ten minutes or so and then bid him adieu and went back into the water.

The swim in had taken longer than expected and Bosun in the dinghy and the rest back on *Seac* were probably wondering where I was. I was in the water but I was exhausted and stumbling around like a drunk every time a wave hit me. Even in the pitch dark I could see that there were several lines of breakers between where I was and where I hoped I'd find Bosun, breakers I'd have to go under. My first try at the waves confirmed what I already knew: You can't dive under a wave wearing a life jacket. I tried again and then I tried to throw myself over the waves, but with no luck. It was decision time. Either I ditch the jacket and drown or I give the job up. It took me no time at all to decide. I turned and climbed up the beach looking for Louis. I gave a passing thought to Bosun in the dinghy, which was in so near the surf line, and to my other comrades back on the boat, all so close to the lee shore, but mostly I was just thankful to be alive and out of the water. Then I realized I was very much alone. Louis was not where I left him on the beach. There had been no time for panic when I was being hammered in the surf but now there was time and I was scared.

I knew the charts and sailing directions for this stretch of coast and I'd heard Mac and Henri talk about it. From Arcachon to the Gironde this was 50 miles of the most desolate and unpopulated coastline in Europe. While I was in the water Louis had plenty of time to dress and was probably a mile away by now, in what direction, who knows. I stood there wet, naked, and lost. And cold. The September wind was icy after the warmer water of the Bay so I started walking down the beach more to get warm than with a destination in mind. There was no town nearby and Hourtin lighthouse was three or four miles away. I dismissed the idea of going there but at the same time I could see the lighthouse-keeper's face, when he opened his door and found a large naked American cast up out of the Bay. It made me chuckle. It was going to be a long stretch before I had anything to chuckle about again.

I stopped for a minute to watch the flash of the lighthouse off the dunes and found myself counting off the five-second intervals when I heard a moan come up from the sand at my feet. I almost fell over Louis, apparently just where I had dumped him earlier, the current having carried me a ways to the north. He was on his knees now, struggling to get into his natty double breasted suit, a suit well soaked in sea water and matted with wet sand. Little Louis wasn't much, but I was never happier to see anyone in my life. I helped him get dressed, buried our life jackets in the sand, and improvised a sort of loincloth for myself out of the Frenchman's T-shirt. Then we turned toward the dunes and in the dark of the moon started walking.

The moors in this part of France are called the Hourtin Downs by the British and are the northern end of the Landes, a vast area of scrub pines extending south almost to the Pyrenees. The sand dunes that rise behind the beach are covered with a tangle of thorns and an occasional tree, stunted and blown bare by the salt winds. We hiked over and around the dunes for more than an hour and I assumed Louis knew where he was going. There was no conversation. I spoke only a few words of French and Louis spoke no English. All we had in common was a bit of Spanish but the words that one of us knew the other couldn't understand. Besides, we had little to talk about.

We came to a dune that loomed above us like a mountain. "*Regardez*," said Louis, pointing upward. With new strength I struggled up the dune, thinking that from here we'd get our bearings and locate a village or at least some place with a telephone so Louis could call his people. From the top the view was discouraging: we were looking back into the Bay of Biscay. We had come full circle and were back about where we started. To the north, south, and east was just solid darkness. Now we couldn't even see Hourtin light.

It was time for me to take over. I pointed to what I was reasonably sure was the North Star, at least a star to our north, and gestured that we'd keep it to our left. This way we'd at least be going in one direction and going inland. Another hour, by celestial navigation, and we came to a foot path running north and south. By gestures I asked Louis which way and he answered with a shrug. Swell, I thought, and we headed south. We were both dead tired; the cold wind was turning me blue and my feet were bleeding. We stopped long enough for me to rip my T-shirt jock strap into two pieces and tie them around my feet. So what if I got frost bite. I couldn't worry now about my future social life, if there was ever to be any.

We headed south for another hour and skirted some salt marshes and a large pond. It seemed like we walked forever before we saw the first evidence there was ever any human existence in this strange wasteland. Running through the pines, west to the beach, we found the ruins of a roadway, a fantasy road out of a dream by Dali. Huge slabs of concrete lay one after the other in a rough line—one connected and each at a different angle in the white sand. A derelict road that began nowhere and led nowhere, it was not a road to be followed. It had been built by the Germans to service their coast defense bunkers on the beach and had probably been bombed. We stuck to our footpath. It was only a little farther along, perhaps a mile, that our path became a single-lane dirt road and we saw the first sign of habitation, an electric light hanging on a pole next to two or three ramshackle corrugated sheds, apparently a lumber camp or a turpentine mill. Louis stopped and talked to me in a worried and serious way. I understood few of the words he spoke but could pretty well read his gestures. In Tangier there was almost never much problem communicating, even with the Arabs. Everyone there spoke bits of French, Spanish, and English and a hybrid patois of all three. Gates had gotten on fine just speaking Italian. But alone with Louis, one on one, it was tougher. He was obviously concerned and let me know we were both in danger, especially me without any identity papers.

The plan was for me to stay out of the way but in the event someone spoke to me I was to act drunk and say nothing. Then he changed the script and suggested I play a deaf mute. He instructed me how to grunt and showed me how he wanted my eyes rolled back to show a maximum of whites. Boy, this will be fun, I thought. He motioned me into the trees and went off to reconnoiter and look for a phone. He was back quickly to report no telephone lines into the camp and there was nobody around. We started walking again until we came to a blacktop road. This would have encouraged us if we hadn't been exhausted to the point of collapse. I was freezing to death, and my feet were bleeding more than ever. On top of this we were still lost. It was obvious that Louis didn't know this part of the country any better than I did; he was a city boy, not a Piney, as we called them back home. The bandages on my feet, the only garments to my name, were fast disintegrating to nothingness. And having done very little walking on *Seac* for a week, my legs were starting to cramp up.

It must have been five o'clock in the morning now and while I'd been looking forward to seeing France I would just as soon have been in the Parade with Nancy, drinking gin. We were moving a lot slower and every so often we'd both lie down in the road to rest. This was a lousy way to spend a night. Smuggling was getting drunk with the boys in the Mar Chico or Dean's, not this crap. Well, I thought, things could hardly get worse. I was wrong of course: right then it started to rain.

"I'll be dipped in shit," I said aloud and in English.

It was coming on dawn, and in the early light I spotted a barn on a hill maybe 50 yards off the road. It was only the third or fourth building we'd seen since the sawmill. With a few gestures, and fewer words, I made it plain to Louis that for me that barn was the end of the line. If he could reach his people and come get me, fine. If the police found me, that would be fine too, but I was done with the hiking and bleeding. Louis elected to go on—he was the one with the shoes and the suit—and I headed across the muddy field to the barn.

CHAPTER 6

Port of the Moon

To call it a barn was stretching a point. It *had* been a barn. Most of its roof had long since given up the ghost and fallen through to the dirt floor. A number of boards were missing on three sides and it had no fourth side. I gathered together all the straw I could find and bedded down in the darkest corner. The straw was little protection against the rain and the cold, but it was something. I had slept for maybe two hours when I was awakened by voices.

Two men were speaking French just outside the barn. Through a gap in the boards I could see they were farmer types, both smoking pipes and one of them carrying a shotgun. At first the sight of the gun caused me some mild alarm, but then I realized that even if they saw my footprints in the mud and followed them into the barn, it was unlikely they'd shoot me. More likely they'd fetch a gendarme. I began to mull over an assortment of stories I might come up with to explain my naked presence. Each scenario got better as I worked on them and I hardly noticed when the farmers walked back to the road. Another hour and a small van stopped on the road and three men got out. Louis was one of them.

On *Seac* Louis was like all the other contact men who had sailed with MacQueen; they were regarded pretty much like one additional item of cargo. A non-person. But here, in his own element and among his own people, Louis was something else. In this part of France Louis was a leader among men, a *chef du contrabande.* Without doubt a transformation had taken place, a sea change, since I last saw Louis.

As soon as I was in the van he snapped an order to the larger of his two companions and without hesitation the man whipped off his trench coat, his sailor's striped jersey and his socks, and handed them to me. We covered some of the same road in the van that we had hiked during the night and Louis told me with a finger count that we had walked about 20 kilometers. It might have been less but still too far to travel barefoot and bare-assed on a cold night.

Sometime that morning we stopped at a farmhouse and sat down to a meal of soup, cheese, and wine. I ate and drank until I was on the edge of a coma. A buxom country lass, the farmer's daughter, was sent to a village to find me some shoes and while she was gone our host served us coffee and brandy and rummaged up a pair of trousers for me. The group then made a combined effort to warn me of the danger I was in should we be stopped by the police, or worse, by the customs people. This was smugglers' country and there were road blocks as well as boat patrols looking to pick up the *contrabandier.* With a bit of French and a bit of Spanish they let me know it was bad enough to be a smuggler but it was double bad to be without any papers at all, an undocumented alien. If we were stopped I was to say nothing and my friends would tell a story of an unfortunate American seaman who had been taken drunk in Bordeaux and missed his ship.

We finished our breakfast, I got my shoes, such as they were, and we were off to the city. Bordeaux, on a crescent bend of the Garonne River, in years past was called the Port of the Moon. In many respects the city resembles New Orleans, but many centuries older. A coincidence, perhaps, that Lafitte of New Orleans, America's most famous smuggler, was born here.

We arrived in the city in mid-afternoon and stopped at our driver's apartment in the old part of town to shave and wash and pick me up a sweater. Walking back to the car it was small wonder I was an object of curiosity. My trousers were the striped kind usually associated with weddings and funerals and had been made for a man much shorter and heavier. They just came to the top of my bright red socks and were tied at the waist with a piece of string. The shoes were blue canvas slippers with yellow straw soles, too small but slit at the sides to accommodate my swollen feet. I returned the trench coat to the man who had given me the shirt off his back and now I wore a baby blue cardigan sweater over my French Navy jersey. I ignored the stares and piled into the van with my new comrades, anxious to get back to the coast and back out to *Seac*. While my party seemed in a hurry when we started, we weren't in such a hurry we couldn't stop at three or four roadside cafés to take care of our thirsts. Wherever we stopped, the people were known to Louis and were trusted. I figured them to be his customers or retailers of his contraband tobacco. At each stop Louis regaled his friends with the story of our night's adventure and demonstrated how I pulled him from the Bay. By the deference they showed me I realized I was the hero of the piece and was also being touted as a big man at the African end of the pipeline.

Our destination now was Arcachon, a fishing port that was also a bit of a local seaside resort. Some of the cafés were closed for the season, but we found one that was open and met two more men from Louis' organization. They told us a heavy surf at the mouth of Arcachon Basin had kept all boats in port for the past five days, hence no contact. None of this crowd, Louis included, seemed too concerned about their inability to perform their part of the operation, and when I thought about the beating *Seac* took coming north and the night I had just spent in the dunes, I boiled over. Despite the language problem I let them know what I thought of them as smugglers and seamen. I also let them know that if they didn't get a boat out to the rendezvous pretty damn soon they needn't bother—Mac, *mon Capitain*, would either dump their stuff in the Bay or would take it home. They heard me and understood and promised another effort but didn't say much more. After a dinner of *mouclade*, mussels in white cream sauce, at an *auberge* on the beachfront, Louis and I and our driver left Arcachon and drove back to Bordeaux.

It was late in the evening when they took me to the Brasserie La Belle Rose. It was on the banks of the Garonne near the town of Carbon-Blanc and was run by Mama and Papa Cazaux, more particularly by Mama. Mama was also a member of Louis' band of smugglers. She was a very large woman, tall and heavy, and bore a striking resemblance to Primo Carnera. She showed me to a bedroom upstairs over the bar and I was hardly asleep when her big paw was shaking me awake again. It was four o'clock and she said it was time to go. I was too tired to argue. I got dressed and followed her downstairs and had a bowl of café au lait in the shuttered kitchen. Then I was in a Citroen full of smugglers and on the road again. We drove up the river, across a bridge into the city and through the deserted Place de la Comedie in front of Bordeaux's magnificent theater. At a street crossing under the hovering walls of the 700-hundred-year-old cathedral a parked truck answered our flash of headlights and pulled out to follow us. On his lap Louis had a cloth flour sack with $40,000 in French, British, and American banknotes.

We were headed this time for a tidal creek a couple of kilometers north of the village of Talais. The same grayish oysterboat that had met *Seac* on the last rendezvous was waiting there for us. The creek had fallen to bare mud with the ebb tide, and the 30-footer lay awkwardly against the bank. We carried cans of gas-oil and paraffin from the truck to the boat, hurrying to get done before it got light. One of the men who came on the truck was Robert, our contact man from the last run. He was in charge of the party that would try to make it to *Seac*. Louis, by gestures, let me know he had had his fill of the sea for awhile and would stay ashore. He gave the bag of money to Robert, gave me an affectionate hug and a bunch of thank-you's and left in the car followed by the truck. I crept into the hold of the boat with Robert and two other men and waited for the tide. After two hours in the wet, smelly boat bottom the tide began to flood the creek and lap against the hull. When we finally felt the boat come afloat, someone started the engine. We raised the hatch a few inches and in the early morning light I saw the bleak mud flats and watched our wake wash crabs off the banks of the creek.

The day had dawned a solid gray: mud flats, river and sky. We bucked a short cross-sea across the Gironde to the north, past Pointe de Grave and on to Pointe de la Coubre where we left our skiff at anchor in a cove. Here the cargo would be put ashore that night and trucked into the city. Then it was into the Bay heading south across the shoals known as the Bank of Olives and past the wreck of a Liberty ship. In the open water the waves were running high and getting steeper as we went.

Butting along I realized our boat was not meant for this sort of work. Instead of riding the long swells, we were slamming into each sea like hitting concrete. Robert and I huddled with the captain from Talais in the wheelhouse, up to our ankles in water. With each jolt we fell against the sides of the cabin and before long boards were coming loose. The damned boat was disintegrating. And things got worse, not better. Robert turned green and lost his morning coffee over the side. Our captain had a change of heart about the whole venture and claimed his engine couldn't operate in such seas. He was probably right but I urged him to continue south. To no avail. We were not much south of the lighthouse of Cordouan when he turned and ran back to Coubre.

Our cove at Coubre was in the lee of sand flats on the west and south and was sheltered on the north by a pine forest. It was noon when we slipped behind the piled sand into the little bay known as Bonne Anse. The tide was running out and we passed five or six dories straining at their anchor lines. The roar of the sea beyond our crescent of white sand seemed strangely distant from the tranquility of the cove.

We beached our boat and it was clear that our rendezvous with *Seac* would have to wait. Robert and one of his men waded ashore and disappeared into the pines in search of a telephone and some food. Surveying the area I saw cement bunkers and blockhouses every fifty yards or so in the woods. More unpleasant reminders of the German occupation. The receding tide left our boat dry on its spit of sand, and hours passed with no sign of Robert. I was having stomach pains for want of food.

To my surprise Robert had left the sack of money with me rather than with the boat captain and I used it now for a pillow as I lay on the deck. Had it occurred to me to take the money and run? It was the first thought I had the minute Robert left it with me. But where to go? I could not speak French and had no papers; the only friends I had in this country were the people I'd be running away from. The idea had its appeal but just wasn't do-able.

I tried to think of all the food I could buy with $40,000 but it didn't make me feel any better. I let the captain know again how hungry I was and this time I got some action. He was apparently hungry too. He took a shovel and bucket onto the beach and spent the next half hour digging in the sand. When he returned he had a good quantity of small clams called *lavagnons*, a delicacy now pretty much limited to this portion of the French coast, that he opened with a jack-knife. I ate like I'd never seen food before. We had hardly finished the clams when Robert and his man came back with bread, oysters, pâté, and wine and we had something of a feast.

They had gone some distance, he said, to find a telephone and report our situation to Louis in Bordeaux. He had also found a café just a hundred yards or so back in the pines of Coubre Forest, the place he'd gotten our lunch. He thought it would be safe for all of us to pay it a visit, but after dark.

At flood tide we moved the boat to deeper water and put out an anchor. After dark we borrowed one of the dories since it wasn't clear what had become of our skiff, and went ashore. The tiny Café de la Côte Sauvage was deserted except for its proprietor and one patron, a lighthouse-keeper from the giant Coubre lighthouse. The five of us off the boat ate omelets and eels in red wine and drank our wine in silence; the other two paid little attention to us except to comment on the bad weather. As there was now a possibility that Louis and more of his band would come out from the city that night, Robert, his two men, and the boat captain arranged to stand watch at the place in the pines where the road ended. I was delighted not to be included. I rowed back to the boat, made myself a bed in the hold in a pile of fishnets, and got my first real sleep since I left *Seac*.

Shortly after dawn they began to arrive; two in a truck, two in the Citroen, a couple more and I lost count. By mid-morning the woods looked like a smugglers' convention. There were free traders everywhere—in the café, on the beach, and asleep in the truck. Everybody was there except Louis who apparently preferred the comforts of Bordeaux to roughing it on "the savage coast." The wind was blowing almost a gale again and there was no hope of getting to sea that day in the boat we had. We spent the day drinking wine and waiting for a bigger and more seaworthy boat that was supposed to be on its way to Coubre. Occasionally someone took a break from the drinking and walked out on the spit of sand to the south to have a

Lighthouse at Coubre Point, France.

look with the glasses. No boat came that day and the storm got worse, as bad as it had been on our way to the rendezvous the week before. The storm blew and the smugglers got drunk and it looked like it was going to be some time before I would see *Seac* again. Robert was in contact with Bordeaux by telephone and the reports we heard at the cove were varied and conflicting. The boat that was supposed to come couldn't get out of Arcachon. No, the boat had gotten out and had reached the rendezvous, but there was no *Seac*. No, the rendezvous had been accomplished and the first load was even now on its way to the Gironde; I would go out when they went for the second load. We waited all day and there was no boat, no rendezvous, and eventually we even stopped getting reports from Bordeaux. That night I slept again in the oyster boat.

The next morning, my fourth in France, we felt some reconnaissance was in order and the Frenchmen got together and worked out a plan. Three of us cleaned ourselves up and hoping we looked like tourists we gained admission to Coubre lighthouse. From the top of the 210-foot lighthouse we saw the full fury of the storm in the Bay and looked anxiously for sight of either the boat that was promised us or *Seac*. There were no boats to be seen. The storm we watched was a renewal of the one that had plagued *Seac* up the Iberian coast and into the Bay and it was later reported to be the worst Atlantic storm in several years. We went back down to our friends in the pines and resumed our drinking. Then the boat came.

The boat was a sturdy forty-foot, sea-going fishing boat out of Arcachon, but berthed now somewhere up the

Gironde. The two men who brought her into the cove looked as seaworthy as their boat and not the type to be disturbed by a little wind and rough water. The man in charge of the boat was a beefy red-faced fellow, and his mate was the saltiest looking character I had yet encountered. The turtleneck sweater he wore was an unexpected snow white and set off his cordovan-colored face. In texture his complexion was a perfect match to the wineskin hanging from his shoulder. There was no question that the man had been to sea forever; here indeed was the Ancient Mariner. They had a drink with us before they left for the harbor at Royan. They had been to the rendezvous, we learned, but they could find no trace of *Seac*. With this disheartening news the rest of us returned to Bordeaux.

I stayed again at the Belle Rose and it was two more days before the storm subsided enough to get even the big boat out into the Bay. Then I was taken to Royan and the men from Arcachon took me out with them for another look at the rendezvous. We held little hope that *Seac* would still be there but we went anyway. It was a long ride out and a longer ride back. There was no *Seac*. The trip, however, was not a total loss; on the way back in, the mate taught me to drink from a wineskin. This, after all, was something.

Instead of a cargo of contraband tobacco, the Bordeaux folks now had an illegal alien on their hands. Having arrived, as I did, unencumbered by worldly goods and with no knowledge of their language, it was as if a foundling had been left on their doorstep. What I had expected might be a one- or two-day stay in France now became something else with the disappearance of *Seac*. The immediate problem was to keep me out of sight and out of trouble until arrangements could be made to return me to my own people.

After discussion, and with some reluctance on Mama Cazaux' part, the Belle Rose was chosen as my hideout. For a café the Belle Rose was a quiet place. It was patronized mostly by neighborhood people who stopped in at noon or maybe in the evening for their aperitif. The meal trade was slow but this was just as well because Mama's kitchen was generally full of smugglers and too much business would have hampered the café's contraband activities. Mama Cazaux was not a relaxed person and she was in constant fear I would be found out. Shuffling around the bar and kitchen in a pair of run-down carpet slippers, a dead fly caught in her grey hair, and picking her teeth with a paring knife, she was constantly after Louis and the others to get me out of there. Papa Cazaux was half her size and was not much of a factor in either the café operation or the cigarette business. He helped with the cooking and the bar but most days he was off with his shotgun and a pair of dogs hunting birds. *La chasse* was what Papa lived for.

But for all her apprehension Mama treated me alright. I ate well, mostly steak, fried potatoes, and cheese and the little birds Papa brought home, whatever they were. I had as much good wine as I wanted. And every couple of days she made a bouillabaisse that was out of this world. Most of the time Mama kept me in the kitchen, in a woodshed in the rear of the place, or in my room upstairs. I got my exercise pacing between the kitchen and woodshed and in the evening I went upstairs and watched ships on the river. At noon each day the local prefect of police stopped by for his two glasses of Pernod and for me this meant an hour in the bedroom. But sometimes in the evening I was able to out-maneuver Mama and sit outside for a little while under the big chestnut tree in front of the café.

The crisp Autumn air was a change from Morocco, but after a few days I was sick of the place and tired of hiding. My hosts were apparently getting a little tired of this, too. Louis left to fly to Tangier to see what could be done to get *Seac* and his cigarettes back to France and to see what could be done with the American. I stayed on at the café while Louis was gone.

There were few diversions, but one was the gypsies. The café was at the fork of two roads and on the route the gypsy tribes took on their way down through the Landes to the Pyrenees and Spain. Some had cars and trucks but most of them travelled in horse-drawn wagons. Often they'd camp overnight by the road junction and sometimes one or two would come into the café for wine.

Better than the gypsies was the circus. I woke up one morning and there they were, setting up in front of the Belle Rose. They had a single round tent with white and red panels and a bunch of beat-up old trucks and vans, an old fashioned one-ring traveling circus. I watched from the front door of the café and by noon I'd seen two elephants, a baboon, three or four chimpanzees, a pony, and a bunch of dogs. That day and the next the bar was full of circus people and Mama loosened up enough to let me join them for a few glasses of wine. The real high point was when the beautiful lady acrobat used my woodshed to wash her clothes. She not only smiled at me but I was sure that on her way out she blew me a kiss. The second night

Mama surprised me and allowed me to go to the performance with one of her boys called YuYu. YuYu was one of Robert's four brothers, pleasant, likeable and very frowzy. All of the brothers were in the gang. The circus was great. The music was an electric organ and a drummer. There were jugglers, clowns, a trapeze act of sorts, a dog and pony act, and my lady acrobat and her partner.

Two nights after the circus Mama surprised me again and let YuYu and another fellow take me into the city for a couple of hours, on condition that we only drink in bars along the riverfront where a foreigner wouldn't arouse curiosity. Mama had really mellowed and I drank that night in some of the meanest, dirtiest saloons in the world.

After a week in the Belle Rose I got word that Louis was coming back from Tangier and I had high hopes of a quick return to Africa. He flew from Tangier to Marseille and took a train from there to Bordeaux and I was allowed to go to the station with YuYu to meet him. YuYu knew about as much Spanish as I did and I was able to communicate with him better than with the rest of them. On the way into the city he told me he had a wife and three children, but this was no deterrent to his life as a smuggler.

As soon as we met Louis in the station I realized my hope of getting out of France in the foreseeable future was a pipe dream. He had not brought my passport and clothes as I expected him to. Too risky, he said, to try to use a passport without a proper entry stamp. Too much depended now on my not getting picked up. I would leave France, he told me, as I had come—I must be smuggled out on *Seac*. MacQueen was even then preparing for another trip north.

"When?" I asked him.

"With the new moon."

Discouraging, this, as we were driving back to the Belle Rose that night under a full moon, the harvest moon. I considered getting out of the car right there on the bridge over the Garonne and trying to find my own way out of their country. Alone and without papers or money couldn't be any worse than another two weeks in the kitchen and woodshed. Back at the café I let them know how I felt and Mama had something new in store: I would leave the next day "for the country."

YuYu took me to the wine farm the next morning. It was maybe 20 miles east of Bordeaux but they never mentioned exactly where we were. Long afterwards I looked at a map, remembered some names on road signs, and concluded we were in the St. Emilion district. No wonder the wine was good. Probably it was part of a chateau, but I never saw the chateau, only the rolling hillsides of grapevines and the one-story stone tenant house. They let me know that this would be my home until *Seac* came back to collect me. Our host was a part-time smuggler, part-time wine grower who lived on the place with his brother and his brother's family. How many of them were ever told the story of how I came to be there I never knew. The lady of the house understood that I was an American seaman who had missed his ship and was YuYu's distant cousin. If the wrong people came to the farm, I thought my best bet would be the deaf-mute thing. A deaf-mute living on a remote farm—it couldn't miss.

The place was pleasant but primitive. An outhouse and a well in the yard, but no indoor plumbing. YuYu and I slept in a room next to the kitchen in massive old beds between corn-shuck mattresses and feather comforters. The stone-floored kitchen was the main room in the house. On the other side, attached to the house, was the cow shed and the wine shed. When the two cows were in for the night they were maybe seven feet from the table where we ate, but smelled a lot closer. The door from the kitchen to the yard stayed open and there was always a parade of small barnyard animals coming in to eat scraps and crumbs off the kitchen floor. They ate well and we ate well. There were plenty of fresh vegetables from the garden and it was only a short time before I worked out a plan for the meat course. I sat in the kitchen in the early afternoon and kept an eye on what came in. First the ducks: There were maybe eleven of them. Then the geese, the chickens, and the rabbits, lots and lots of rabbits. When I saw something that looked good, I gave the cook a yell and pointed. The system worked, to a point. Too seldom I got a duck or a goose, too often I got a rabbit. After the rabbit dishes of our nine-cent lunches in Tangier, I thought I'd never again eat anything called *lapin*, but these were the real item and we ate an awful lot of our self-replenishing little friends. For nine or ten meals a week it was rabbit roasted, rabbit fried, and rabbit fricassee. What our meals lacked in variety they made up in freshness. There were times we were eating our soup as some luckless bunny was being skinned outside the door. I looked at more than one dish of stew waiting to see a twitch.

Despite the fact we were guests, YuYu and I helped with the work. When the grape harvest began, the whole household was up at dawn, and after some coffee, bread, and cheese we took to the vineyards with baskets and shears. The weather was fine for a change, and there was laughing and singing as men, women, and children worked through the rows of vines. The small baskets were emptied into larger baskets that men carried on their backs to wooden vats on oxcarts where the grapes were run through a hand-cranked crusher. Then the vats were hauled down to the shed on the side of the house for the pressing. In the evening we all helped tighten down the big screw press and made wine. In two short months I was learning two new trades.

The days spent in the vineyards were sunny and pleasant and went by a lot quicker than the days spent hiding in La Belle Rose. In the evening when we were done with the pressing, we ate roasted chestnuts and drank wine. On a Saturday night we drove in YuYu's car to a little crossroads café and stayed out most of the night drinking and dancing. The pastoral life, the crisp October days and the evenings with my friends—it was all great fun but something was missing. What I missed, I realized, was hot, noisy, smelly Tangier.

Then the day came when we finished the wine harvest. The last cartload of grapes came down from the hillside with a bunch of flowers fastened to the oak vat and garlands around the necks of the oxen. We stayed up the whole night sampling the barrels of last year's vintage and sipping some of the new wine that was still in the making. Week-old wine is rich and sweet and not much to my taste compared with the real stuff, but it was a great seasonal treat to my hosts. By the time the sun rose behind the vineyards, though, it began to taste pretty good.

The sun wasn't up long before a little Renault pulled into the yard and we got the word we were wanted back in the city. The Boss Charlie, I was told, had arrived from Tangier and would direct the business of making our rendezvous with *Seac*.

That evening we went from the farm to YuYu's place on the north outskirts of Bordeaux. YuYu lived in a fantastic pile that had once been a very grand chateau but was now in a state of epic dilapidation. Its walls, cracked with the years, still showed a reluctance to crumble completely. A sinister tangle of weeds and ivy reached up to the shuttered windows on the second floor and a great oak door hung askew on one hinge. An inside courtyard was lit by a single bulb dangling from the railing on the flight of stone steps that led up to YuYu's upstairs apartment. YuYu had five rooms and each one was more cavernous than the one before. The dining hall was 50 feet long, and a massive old mahogany table, four or five chairs, and a stained and torn portrait of someone in a uniform were its only furnishings. The bedroom I slept in that night was like the nave of Chartres Cathedral.

The next morning I met with the Boss Charlie—and . . . no surprise, it was Charlie Miranda. We sat at one end of the long table, had a drink of wine, and Charlie filled me in on details Louis had failed to bring back with him from Tangier. He told me of the vigil Bosun had kept in the dinghy on that September night so long ago and how *Seac* had finally returned to Africa through the storm with the men on half rations. I heard how the word spread in Dean's and the Parade that *Seac* was back one man short and that the American had either drowned or been shot to death in a gunfight at the rendezvous. I chuckled with

Charlie about the stories but only a little bit. *Seac* had been overhauled and was on its way north as we were talking. I said I was glad to hear it.

"How have these people been treating you?" he asked.

"They've been OK," I said, "They've been good to me, but I'm damned well fed up with France and all the time hiding."

"They've got reason to treat you good, kid," Charlie said. "Louis told us how you pulled him out of the surf and saved his ass. But the hiding, that's necessary. I'm laying low myself while I'm here. This is the first time in three days I've been out of the hotel. The heat is really on. Maybe you didn't hear about the deal with the airplane." I said I hadn't.

"Some damned fool in Tangier—some new guy—he got the bright idea to bring over some gold in an airplane, you know, one of those little single-engine jobs. He loads the plane with gold, gets across the Med, and then crashes his machine outside of Toulouse. All this just less than a week ago. The cops didn't have to be too damned clever to figure out where the guy came from. Now every cop and customs guy in France is out looking for smugglers, out looking to pick up anybody who has even heard of Tangier. So you see, you gotta stay out of the way until Mac gets here, only a couple of days now."

"I've been here nearly a month already," I complained, "and I'm going nuts. I don't even have the price of a drink in my pocket." He dug into his wallet and handed me a couple of 1000 franc notes. I thanked him, but without much enthusiasm. "I'd let you have more, kid, you know that, but it wouldn't be good you should get picked up and have a roll on you. Anyway, you ain't going nowhere to spend money, just back to *Seac.* You need anything, you just tell these people, hear? Its not just you, we all gotta take orders. You take orders from Mac, he's your boss. Me, I gotta take orders too, from my boss. We all got a boss."

I wanted to ask him who *his* boss was, but thought better of it. Instead I asked him if there was any other news from Tangier. "*The Great Scot,*" he said, "I guess you didn't hear, no, there was no way you could. Martin sold her to Caulfield from Gib, you probably knew that. Well, she was in a gunfight south of Naples and the Italians got her." I asked whether they got Serge, but he didn't know.

Café et Restaurant de la Côte Sauvage, France.

Chapter Seven

The Savage Coast

After my meeting with Charlie, YuYu took me over to La Belle Rose. I agreed to go only with the assurance it would be for one night only. Not just my last night at the Belle Rose, they told me, my last night in France. Tomorrow we would meet *Seac*. From my old room overlooking the river I looked at the waning moon for a couple of minutes and then went to sleep. Mama woke me at three in the morning. I dressed quickly this time and got down to the kitchen where Mama had the blinds drawn and was drinking coffee with Louis and YuYu. It was like old times. Before we left the kitchen and went through the back gate to a car, Mama handed Louis the now familiar sack of money. I said my final goodbye to Mama, and we were on our way.

It was still dark when we got to Arcachon and met a man in front of the Moorish casino in the town center. We were greeted with the news that the boat that was supposed to take us out had broken down. Another boat, we were promised, would be along soon. We waited.

Just before noon we were told we would have our boat shortly—just as soon as it came back in from a day of fishing. Other than me, no one seemed too upset about this. If there was one thing these Frenchmen had, and I lacked, it was patience. I began to wonder if the French smuggler wasn't maybe being paid by the hour. I tried to make the best of it and enjoy the windy, sunny day. The town had the lazy emptiness of a resort out of season. We had a good dinner at noon at a little place near the boat basin starting with a dozen of the flat oysters the town was famous for—better than belons, better than any other oysters in the world. Afterwards we had some rum and played cards. It was dark again before we got together with our boat.

We met the boat at the southeastern end of Arcachon Basin near the little hamlet of Le Teich. We parked the car in some trees and carried baskets of food and wine over to the beach. This was for *Seac* and I made sure they had it this time. We also had some food for ourselves. We had a shotgun with us, too, I noticed. After a few minutes we heard the chug-chug of our boat coming up the channel, but it was too black to see anything. The moon was a few nights short of a new moon, but now it was clouded over. When it sounded like the boat might run aground at our feet, Louis lit a match and held it in front of his face. Instead of scaring the pilot back to sea, as I thought it might, the face in the dark served to guide the boat to a stop near where we were standing. The boat showed no light of any kind, something I was used to now. We felt our way aboard with our stuff, and the man at the helm reversed his motor and swung out through a cluster of small boats that were anchored there. Someone in the bow called out steering directions in a low voice as we made our way down the narrow channel between a couple of sand islands with maybe thirty inches of water under us. It was still too dark to see much of the boat or the men on it. YuYu's hand kept my shoulder down on the deck, and we lay still until we had cleared the anchorage. Finally a sliver of moon gave just enough light to see that the boat was similar to the one I was on with the Ancient Mariner and his mate, maybe a little smaller. There were fish holds fore and aft and no cabin. There looked to be two men aboard besides the three of us from the Belle Rose.

We headed west past the island in the center of the bay and then turned south to the mouth of the Basin. Moving through the water, we had a nice supper of pâté, cheese, and red wine. The salt air and the prospect of rejoining *Seac* gave me an appetite, and I ate and drank more than my share. I knew this soon enough when we got near the sand banks across the mouth of the bay and the water started kicking up. It was really blowing out there.

There were mountains of sand to the east, including the largest dune in Europe, low sand shoals to the west, and dead ahead there was a white ribbon of surf breaking on the sand banks called Banc du Nord, Banc du Sud, and Banc d'Argun. The thin moon was behind the clouds again and the five-second red flash of the light to the north of the inlet on Cape Ferret made the spray and foam look like blood. The only other light was from the shower of red and yellow sparks from our exhaust stack.

We were all cold and wet now and I was unpleasantly conscious of my full stomach. I was huddled down deep in a borrowed pea-jacket trying to nap when we ran aground. We hit the sandbar with a jolt and I skidded down the deck ripping out the seat of my pants, my lovely striped formal wear. I hung on to some part of the boat but I was in water to my chest. Somebody near me was completely in the water and I didn't have to know the language to know he was saying he couldn't swim. I caught his arm and helped him back into the boat. Good God, I thought, somebody is going to get killed yet. Our bow was pointing almost straight up and at the same time the boat was lying on its side. Before we hit the sand, things had been quiet. Now the night air was full of shouts and curses. The food and wine we had for *Seac* was gone over the side. And I had broomed *Antonina* because I thought it too risky, that I might get my ass in a jam. At that moment I had no trouble at all seeing Lacey and his boys laying off Cap d'Antibes sipping champagne with French ladies in bikinis.

We'd lost our baskets of provisions but we still had the shotgun and the bag of money. To that extent we were still in business, if a capsized boat on a sand shoal can be said to be in business. Nobody had much of an idea how to get us off and we might still be there but for the grace of God and a monster wave that broke on us and spun us back into deep water.

Running aground had damaged both our steering gear and our pilot's spirits. He argued with Louis for turning around and going home. Since my first trip out of Talais, my ear was tuned for this and although I didn't relish any further delay, I wasn't too adamant either. For the sake of my ailing stomach I thought maybe a short time-out might be alright. We turned around and headed back up Arcachon Basin. We anchored in a cove at Lège on the north side of the bay and they worked on the steering problem while we waited for the tide to turn. Again I found some fish nets in the hold and curled up for a little sleep. At dawn we lifted anchor and tried again. But this time when we got to the sandbar the breaking seas were enormous and clearly we had no chance of getting out. As we turned inshore for the second time, I saw my first Customs boat.

We might have been fairly inconspicuous if YuYu hadn't been in the bow with his shotgun shooting at seagulls. The white government boat swung over for a closer look and I was sent below decks with Louis. We had too many men aboard for a working fishing boat. The boat passed within a dozen yards of us and peeking from the hatchway I caught a glimpse of a uniformed figure in her bow. For a moment, as they passed, I remembered my first morning in the barn near Hourtin, but now the thought of being caught struck me differently. I had played the game out too far to be caught now. The greatest adventure I looked forward to now was getting back to *Seac* and some dry clothes.

In the early morning we pulled in beneath a pier in the village of Lanton, and Louis and YuYu found us a café. It was a little place sitting between the water and the pine forest and empty at that hour of the morning. Just the place for three weary smugglers to take their rest. I tried to get across to the proprietor the idea of an American breakfast: *oeufs*, *jambon,* and so forth, but to no avail. We had coffee, cheese, and cognac. We played cards 'til noon when Papa Cazaux picked us up and drove us back to La Belle Rose. Mama's raving and ranting about our failure to make the rendezvous was so loud and prolonged I was glad to have an early supper and slip away to my room. This time she woke me at two, and each time I stayed there reveille came earlier. I had my bread and coffee, we took our bag of money, and Louis and I took off once more, two tired and unhappy people. This trip was to the Gironde and it was a cold, nasty day. It was raining when we were in the car and when we got to the estuary it was whipped to a froth by gusts and squalls.

The boat this time was small but at least it had a little cabin with a couple of bunks. The boat's captain was a man new to me, a trim fellow with a crew cut, horned rimmed glasses, and a suit of oilskins that looked like they were from L. L. Bean. A real Princeton type. We bounced out into the Gironde and set a course past Pointe de Grave for the Cordouan light. The first lighthouse out here, miles to the west of the river inlet, was built by the Black Prince in the fourteenth century and at one time there was a small village on the island. Now there was nothing but a cluster of rocks and a 200-foot tall lighthouse. At the light we headed south. It was alright for awhile but then with a wind shift the cabin filled up with engine fumes, and I was forced to spend the rest of the voyage on deck in the rain. We plunged through higher and higher seas, rolling and bouncing until we were abeam of the wrecked Liberty ship and then past it southwest into the Bay.

Early afternoon we reached the rendezvous, at least it was the rendezvous according to Louis. No *Seac*. We seemed to be north of what I remembered of the last rendezvous, but Louis said a new spot had been charted when he was in Tangier. We moved around in various patterns the rest of the afternoon, but there was not another boat in sight. Then we headed back.

We tied up in a fishing village somewhere on the north side of the Gironde, and I walked to Princeton's cottage. He and his wife had a snug place with a blazing fire on the hearth and a simmering kettle of fish soup. The fire and the meal were more than welcome, but I was in no mood, and in no shape, to socialize. The straw soles of my shoes had fallen off, the seat was ripped out of my fancy pants, and I had a five-day growth of dirty beard. I ate my supper and looked at the front page of a Bordeaux newspaper. With my few words of French I recognized a story about the crashed gold plane, a report on the French war in Indochina, and something about fighting in Korea that apparently involved American troops.

YuYu and one of his brothers came to pick us up in a truck, a creaking old wreck well past retirement age, even for old smuggling trucks. I speculated on how many loads of illegal cigarettes it had carried over these coast roads in its day. The truck coughed and wheezed but we bumped our way back to Bordeaux and the Belle Rose. It was almost dawn when we got there and still pouring rain.

The neighborhood by the river was all fast asleep except for Mama's place. Charlie Miranda was there and so were just about all the smugglers I had seen since I was in France. Everyone was excited and there was lots of conversation in French I couldn't understand. Charlie said we didn't stay out in the ocean long enough and that *Seac* was out there waiting for us. How he knew this he didn't say. "I have you a boat now that will stay out for a week, if that's what it takes. A month—whatever."

What a happy thought that was. There were a number of things I wanted to say to Charlie, but instead I headed up the stairs in the direction of my nice warm, dry bed.

"And where the hell are you going?" roared Charlie.

Some very smart-ass answers occurred to me but I merely said, "To bed—I'm goin' to bed, that's where I'm going."

"You are like Hell," he said, "You're going out on that boat I got us and you're going out now." I was wrong, of course, about bed, and Charlie was right that I was bound for yet another boat ride. An hour after sun-up I was climbing aboard the fishing boat *Saint Pierre.* They were almost all *Saint Pierre*s, these French fishing boats, but this one was the biggest boat we had yet. Louis and I went aboard around Arcachon somewhere with the usual baggage of wine and food and the bag of money. I went below. The hold of the boat was one long open compartment; two bunks forward, a fish hold amidships, and the engine aft. I got into a bunk and for a minute before I fell asleep I watched a man far to the rear play a blowtorch over the engine to warm it up.

When I woke and went on deck we were in the open Bay. The wind was down, the sea was calmer and the rain was now just a drizzle. Louis was in the wheelhouse looking at a chart. "This is the rendezvous," Louis insisted, "*Ici, ici.*" If this was the rendezvous where the Hell was *Seac?* Then somebody spotted a boat, hull down on the northern horizon. She was coming our way and did look like *Seac.* Louis was squealing now, "*Oui, oui, oui,*" and "*Seac, Seac, Seac.*"

For a minute I believed it myself and when Louis opened a bottle of wine I joined him in a toast. Then we saw we were drinking to just one more fishing boat out of the Gironde. "*Merde,*" we both said, more or less in unison. I tossed the wine bottle into the water and went below again. I felt like crying and damn near did. It was another hour and there was more excitement—Louis had spotted another boat. I watched it come closer and my hopes were up again. I should have known better. It was the same French fishermen, this time on another course. I guess I liked Louis, but I was looking at him now wondering why I ever pulled him out of the Bay. To my mind all this mess was somehow his fault.

I was in my bunk and had dozed off when Louis was down the ladder again, jumping around and jabbering. I tried to kick him in the stomach, but missed. I sat up ready to try again when our boat gave a shudder followed by bumping and scraping noises. Ten seconds later Bosun came down the ladder grinning like an idiot. I followed him over the side onto *Seac* and was greeted by Henri, Pierre, Tony, and Captain MacQueen. Then, for the first and only time on *Seac*, I gave what amounted to an order: "Gentlemen, let's get the crap off-loaded and get the goddamned poker game going."

John with telescope.

Farewell.

Epilogue

[Although John's smuggling days had come to an end, he did follow up his adventures with a brief history of subsequent events and characters he had met in Tangier.]

Antonina saw some good times and some bad times. She came back to Tangier from Villefranche and made some cigarette runs and a couple of trips to Gib and the Canaries with legitimate cargo. No trips to Mecca and none to South America.

Her problems started when Lacey took being Captain a little too seriously. He first insisted that his crew address him properly by the title he'd waited so long to achieve and then insisted that they not leave the mess table until after he did. A little bit of this got old in a hurry and after two trips both the Frenchman and the Irishman quit. Then, once the boat generated some profits, Lacey took off for an extended holiday in London for "drinking and wenching," as Yates put it. When Lacey was slow to return, Yates made Tony Townsend the new captain. After one more successful trip, *Antonina* was snatched from her berth in Tangier by a New Zealander who took her to Gib and wrecked and sank her.

The MacQueens fared somewhat better. They picked up their new boat in Italy, a former minesweeper, and brought her back to Tangier. With *Antonina* gone, Lacey was looking for a berth and Mac took him on again as Mate. On her first trip, a Mediterranean run this time,

Mac set out with food and supplies for three weeks. The boat broke down and drifted off the coast of Tunisia for six weeks. When Mac and his crew were finally rescued they were alive but very hungry and thirsty. After repairs the boat returned to Tangier and made a number of successful cigarette runs.

And finally there was the *Combinatie* affair. Just after midnight on October 2, 1952, the 300-ton Dutch registered motor ship *Combinatie* departed Tangier with 2,700 cases of cigarettes and a manifest for Malta. The ship was owned by an American named Rue Wright and was chartered to a Signor Pedemonte, a cigarette trader who travelled with both Italian and Argentine passports. As soon as the vessel cleared Cape Malabata, it was followed by the 60-ton motor-launch *Esme*. This vessel, also of Dutch registry and a former British sub chaser, was chartered to "Nylon" Sid Paley and Elliot Forrest, supposedly for the purpose of salvaging a similar craft disabled off Malta with a cargo of cigarettes. In addition to its regular captain and crew, *Esme* carried Forrest and three others. At one a.m. on October 4, about 16 miles off the east coast of Spain, *Combinatie* was rammed by *Esme* and boarded by a party of masked men armed with sub-machine guns. The captain and crew of the *Combinatie* were handcuffed, locked in the hold, and taken as prisoners to the French coast near Marseille, where Forrest went ashore and met Paley. When Forrest returned, the ship proceeded to Corsica and near Ajaccio made rendezvous with a smaller launch and off-loaded its cargo. On October 15, after *Combinatie* had been abandoned by its captors, its captain and crew freed themselves and reported the incident. The International Police in Paris began a search for Paley and Forrest.

Sid Paley was arrested by Interpol in Madrid a few weeks later. In December, under an old treaty between the United States and the Sultan of Morocco, he was tried for piracy by the U.S. Consular Court in a courtroom set up in the dining room of the Legation in Tangier. Tony Townsend, described by the *New York Times* as "a scraggly bearded Australian sea captain," testified for the prosecution and linked Paley both to Forrest and the Lucky Luciano organization. Tony said he had been with Paley in the Hotel Excelsior in Rome on several occasions and heard Paley discuss the planning of the job and later say that Forrest had "taken another ship." Townsend acknowledged that he had been working for Paley as captain of the *Laloun* after *Antonina* was sunk. During the trial Townsend was himself being held in a Tangier jail pending another piracy charge, this against a similar craft, the *Rifrock*.

Andrew MacQueen testified for the prosecution that Forrest, on more than one occasion, "had suggested in his own American way" that Mac should get smart and start hijacking his cargoes, rather than buying them.

Charlie Miranda, described by the Associated Press and Reuters as "an American exporter," also testified, as did a Moroccan Jew, an Italian maritime agent, a stateless Pole, a stateless Sudetan, a French ship-owner, and Rue Wright. Testimony was taken in Spanish, English, and French. There was enough mention of Luciano to impel him to hold a press conference in Italy as the trial was proceeding. Said Lucky, "I ain't no cigarette smuggler and I'm disgusted with all that kinda talk."

Paley was found guilty and sentenced to three years in a Federal Penitentiary. He was later re-tried and sentenced to three years probation and a $6,500 fine.

Elliot Forrest, recognized from an Interpol circular, was arrested in the village of Cabriere d'Aigue in France on January 20, 1954. For eight months he had been living in a farm house posing as a deaf-mute writer. In February 1956, Forrest was tried in Marseille for smuggling, along with Charlie Miranda and Sid Paley in absentia. In pre-trial hearings he admitted his raid on *Combinatie* and that he had planned the venture with Paley. He was found guilty and sentenced to three years in a French prison. Paley and Miranda were also convicted and sentenced to eighteen months each.

John Moore (back row on left) with friends.

Afterword

John's last trip, which included his being stranded in France enjoying the "hospitality" of its citizens, seemed to allay his desire for more adventure. His good luck had filled his glass to overflowing. He received a grand sendoff from the *Seac* crew and traveled to Italy (to see the Pope) and thence throughout Europe. He finally headed home in

John Moore in the Army at Camp Rucker, Alabama.

response to a query by his Local Draft Board as to his whereabouts, for this was now the Korean War period.

John arrived back in the States early in January, 1951, and was inducted into the U. S. Army on January 23. He was assigned to a program of instruction as an Army Discussion Leader and deployed to the Counter Intelligence Corps at Camp Rucker, Alabama. John's duties there included conducting investigations, preparing records and courts-martial materials, and indoctrinating troops in the Uniform Code of Military Justice. Honorably discharged in May, 1952, he married his fiancé Marg, and found employment as a sales supervisor and consultant for New Jersey Bell Telephone, while taking evening courses in law at Seton Hall University School of Law. He was awarded his law degree in 1957 and then joined the firm of Pitney, Hardin, and Ward as an Associate Attorney, where he specialized in contracts, anti-trust legislation, commercial claims, corporate affairs, and labor relations. He was a law secretary for superior court Judge Alexander P. Waugh and then became a partner for 35 years in his own firm of Moore and Howell, where he was a trial attorney and civil and criminal defense attorney, defending every type of criminal (with the exception of smugglers), especially the underprivileged and downtrodden. John was also admitted to practice before the United States Supreme Court.

John and I remained close friends. We would often meet for the famous football games at Princeton, where he was the life of the party.

After his retirement in 1993, he continued to remain active as a volunteer orderly at the Lyons Veteran Hospital, Lyons, New Jersey. John passed away on December 3, 1996, deeply mourned.

William F. Haynes, Jr., M.D.

Glossary

Afterdeck: The part of the boat abaft midships.

Atlas Mountains: A mountain range extending across the northwestern portion of Africa, from southern Morocco to the coast of Algiers and Tunisia, for a distance of around 1400 km.

Auberge: An inn (French).

Bangers: A local dish of sausage and mashed potatoes.

Belons: A dish of large and tasty species of oyster, found mainly in Brittany but ranging from the coast of Norway to Morocco.

Berber: A tribe of native or indigenous people who live mostly in Northwest Africa.

Binnacle: A case holding a compass, on board a vessel.

Bints: A slang expression for girl or woman.

Burgee: A triangular flag flown from the mast of a vessel indicating membership in a club or organization.

Burnoose: A woolen cloak usually worn over the shoulder (Berber).

Casbah: The old city.

***Chef de contraband*:** The head of a band of smugglers (French).

***Contrabandier, Contrabandista*:** Smugglers (Spanish).

***Djellaba*:** An outer robe usually with a hood, worn by men and women as protection against the sun (Arabic).

E-boat: A type of German torpedo boat that was referred to as E-boats by the Allies in World War II. The "E" stands for enemy.

Gib: An abbreviated form of Gibraltar.

Guardia Civilis**:** The Spanish police force.

Harry Duffy: A harbor-duty craft akin to an MFV (q.v.).

Fairmile: A type of British torpedo boat MTB (q.v.).

Flamenco: A vigorous dance performed by Andalusian gypsies that has become known among dancers for its energy.

Forepeak: The front area of a vessel at the angle made by the bow, and usually used as storage.

Hawkhurst: A notorious band of smugglers active in the mid-1700s, based in the town of Hawkhurst in the southeastern area of England (Kent and Sussex), who traded with the French.

Hedge anchor: A small anchor used to move a vessel by pulling on its cable (also known as kedge anchor).

Istiqlal movement: Dominant party of the Moroccan Nationalist Movement (1943-56).

Kif: A local hashish.

Lavagnons: A type of clam (French).

Levanter: A strong east wind that blows through the Straits of Gibraltar from time to time.

Majoun: A jam made from cannabis.

Mar Chico: A section of Tangier in which there were numerous bars.

Med: An abbreviated form for Mediterranean.

MFV: Motor fishing vessel.

Mistral: A strong wind blowing through the eastern Mediterranean.

Mouclade: A dish of mussels, often served with white cream sauce.

MTB: Motor torpedo boat.

Muezzin: The Muslim who cries out the hour for daily prayers for the faithful.

Octoroon: A person of mixed descent, in Africa, usually one great grandparent African and seven great grandparents who were white.

Oud: A lute made of wood with six double strings.

Owlers: Another term for smugglers, used in medieval times, perhaps referring to smugglers who usually worked in the night.

Painter: A rope in the bow of a dinghy or small vessel that enables it to be towed or secured.

Rattenbury, Jack: A notorious English smuggler during the early 1800s, known as the "Rob Roy of Devon."

Red Duster: Britain's merchant ensign (flag).

Rif country: A part of the Atlas Mountains (q.v.) where hashish is grown.

Romney Marsh: A picturesque marshland area in the southeast of England in the counties of Kent and East Sussex.

Scorpions: A British term for a type of yacht used in the smuggling trade.

***Seac*:** The *Seac* was an MFV (q.v.) captained by Andrew MacQueen.

S.E.A.C.: South East Asia Command.

Sheila(s): Woman (women) (Berber).

Shilha: Arabic name for Moroccan Berber dialects.

Shipchandler: A dealer in supplies—ropes, sails—for sailing vessels.

Simsar: A pest who deals in nothing more than knowing people or situations, and acting as a professional go-between.

Soco Chico: The area or district known as the heart of Tangier.

Soco Grande: The area next to the Soco Chico.

S.S.: *Schutzstaffel* (German, meaning shield formation). A special unit of the armed forces in Nazi Germany, associated with the some of the worst crimes committed during World War II.

Wasserman test: A test for syphilis.

Wehrmacht: The German (Nazi) Army during World War II, originally designed as the "home defense" of the nation after 1919.